CONFESSING
OUR FAITH

JOHN P. BURGESS

CONFESSING OUR FAITH

The *Book of Confessions*
for Church Leaders

WJK WESTMINSTER
JOHN KNOX PRESS
LOUISVILLE · KENTUCKY

© 2018 John P. Burgess

First edition
Published by Westminster John Knox Press
Louisville, Kentucky

18 19 20 21 22 23 24 25 26 27—10 9 8 7 6 5 4 3 2 1

Book design by Drew Stevens
Cover design by Lisa Buckley Design

Library of Congress Cataloging-in-Publication Data

Names: Burgess, John P., 1954– author.
Title: Confessing our faith : the Book of Confessions for church leaders / John P. Burgess.
Description: Louisville, KY : Westminster John Knox Press, 2018. | Identifiers:
    LCCN 2017049189 (print) | LCCN 2017050621 (ebook) | ISBN 9781611648447 (ebk.) |
    ISBN 9780664503116 (pbk. : alk. paper)
Subjects: LCSH: Presbyterian Church (U.S.A.). Book of confessions. | Presbyterian Church
    (U.S.A.)—Creeds. | Christian leadership.
Classification: LCC BX8969.5 (ebook) | LCC BX8969.5 .B87 2018 (print) |
    DDC 238/.5137—dc23
LC record available at https://lccn.loc.gov/2017049189

CONTENTS

ACKNOWLEDGMENTS

This book has emerged out of classes that I have taught on the confessions for more than two decades at Pittsburgh Theological Seminary. I am thankful to the many students who have engaged this material and helped me shape it for publication. I am also thankful to several colleagues in ministry who read and critiqued the manuscript at an early stage: Lynn Cox, elder and staff member at Eastminster Presbyterian Church (Pittsburgh, PA); James Goodloe, minister and director of the Foundation for Reformed Theology (Richmond, VA); and Trent Hancock, pastor at Glenshaw Presbyterian Church (Pittsburgh, PA), who also helped formulate the study questions for each chapter.

At Westminster John Knox Press, I have been blessed by the enthusiastic support and skillful editorial leadership of David Dobson, who waited patiently (and far too long, I fear) for me to complete the book. As with all my writing, my wife, Deb, has made important suggestions for improvement and assisted with proofreading. Any errors that remain are, of course, my own.

The Presbyterian Church (U.S.A.) has faced difficult challenges in recent years, but its confessional basis remains solid if we will but pay attention to it. I pray that this book will make a modest contribution to renewing the spiritual and theological life of the denomination that first nurtured me in Christian faith and then ordained me to Christian ministry. The church's confessions and the theological traditions that they represent have shaped my own life to the core.

To God be the glory!

HOW TO USE THIS BOOK

This book is designed to give readers maximum flexibility in its use. While I include many key quotations from, and references to, the church's confessions, readers will also benefit by having an up-to-date copy of the *Book of Confessions* close at hand.[1] The book begins with an introduction that describes the responsibilities of church leaders for the *Book of Confessions*. The first chapter proceeds to discuss the meaning of "confession" and to set each of the twelve documents of the *Book of Confessions* into historical and theological context; the next eleven chapters develop some of the confessions' major teachings; and the conclusion challenges church leaders, as grounded in the confessions, to serve as the church's theological and spiritual leaders.

A note about language: Many of the confessions use masculine pronouns for God and humanity (e.g., "men"). When quoting, I have not changed the historic language unless the church has adopted

---

1. In the text, I refer to particular sections of the confessions by paragraph number (e.g., SC 3.01 for the first article of the Scots Confession). See the *Book of Confessions* (Louisville, KY: The Office of the General Assembly, Presbyterian Church (U.S.A.), 2016).

an inclusive language version. While I have sought to use inclusive language as much as possible in my own text, I too occasionally use masculine pronouns for God in order to avoid awkward sentence constructions and to emphasize God's personal character.

The chapters devoted to the confessions' major teachings follow the order of many traditional Reformed confessions: the authority of Scripture, the three persons of the Trinity and the work especially associated with each (for the Father, creation and covenant; for the Son, salvation from sin; and for the Holy Spirit, sanctification and the church), the sacraments, God's consummation of history, and church and society.

Each chapter opens with a brief scenario—a discussion among four church leaders about the confessions and what they have to teach us—followed by an explication of what the confessions say. The conclusion of each chapter returns readers to the concerns of the opening dialogue and offers questions for personal reflection or group discussion. Study leaders and groups may, of course, formulate their own questions for discussion.

While later chapters of this book build on earlier ones, readers are free to read selected chapters or to study them in a different order. A group that wishes to focus on the responsibilities of church leaders could discuss just the introduction and the conclusion. Alternatively, study groups that wish to explore the confessions' major teachings may decide to read only the central eleven chapters. Some groups may wish to study one chapter of the book each week over the course of several weeks or months. Another approach would be for a study leader to ask group members at one meeting to discuss the opening scenario of a particular chapter and then have them read the rest of the chapter at home and discuss it at their next meeting.

ABBREVIATIONS

AC 2.1–2.3   Apostles' Creed (second–eighth centuries)

BSF ##1–80   A Brief Statement of Faith (1991)

C67 9.01–9.56   Confession of 1967 (1967)

CB 10.1–10.9   Confession of Belhar (1982)

DB 8.01–8.28   Theological Declaration of Barmen (1934)

G-x.xxxx   Form of Government, in *Book of Order* (2017–19)

HC 4.001–4.129   Heidelberg Catechism (1562)

KJV   King James Version

NC 1.1–1.3   Nicene Creed (325, 381)

q(q).   question(s)

RSV   Revised Standard Version

SC 3.01–3.25   Scots Confession (1560)

SH 5.001–5.260   Second Helvetic Confession (1561)

W-x.xxxx   Directory for Worship, in *Book of Order* (2017–19)

WC 6.001–6.193   Westminster Confession of Faith (1646)

WLC 7.111–7.306   Westminster Larger Catechism (1648)

WSC 7.001–7.110   Westminster Shorter Catechism (1648)

INTRODUCTION

THE RESPONSIBILITY
OF CHURCH LEADERS FOR
THE *BOOK OF CONFESSIONS*

Opening Prayer: *Holy and merciful God, you call us to declare who we are, what we believe, and what we resolve to do as followers of Jesus Christ. May we confess our faith in a way that deepens our commitment to you and to the life and witness of your church. We pray in Jesus' name. Amen.*[1]

Martha: All four of us will be ordained as elders or deacons on Sunday, and when I think about the vows that we will be taking, well, I don't know about you, but I wonder whether I'm really ready.

Jerry: I was thinking about that too, how we as church leaders are making commitments to know the Bible, the church's confessions, and the church's Form of Government. That's a tall order.

Lisa: I find the *Book of Confessions* especially hard to get into. Some of the confessions use words and ideas that I have never encountered before.

1. Based on chapter 2 of the Form of Government, "The Church and Its Confessions," G-2.0100 and G-2.0500b.

Max: And are these documents from so long ago even relevant today? It may be interesting to know what people
believed in the past, but does it make any difference
for the practical business that we will be transacting?

People called to office in the Presbyterian Church (U.S.A.) — ministers, elders, and deacons alike — take a series of vows when they
are ordained. These vows commit them to knowing and using the
Bible and the church's confessions. But just as the Bible is complex, so too is the *Book of Confessions*. It is not easy to pick it up
on our own. How the different confessions work together to offer
a coherent understanding of the essential tenets of the Reformed
faith is not immediately clear, and their language is sometimes
antiquated and confusing.[2]

Leader training often takes a historical approach to the confessions. In that case, we describe the social and religious context in
which each confession was written and identify the specific issues
of faith to which it was responding. This approach reminds us that
the confessions come from times and places other than our own. So,
while we may sometimes be able to draw parallels between their
affirmations and what we need to confess today, we will also be
aware of our distance from them. We will likely use different words.

As valuable as history is, this book takes a different approach.
While appreciating the historical character of the confessions, it
focuses on the major theological themes that run through them.
And rather than explicating each confession individually, this book
aims at providing a reliable guide to the *Book of Confessions* as a
whole. Readers will receive an introduction to key affirmations of
the Christian faith as developed by the Reformed tradition up to
the present day. This book is a little primer in the basic beliefs that
we hold as Christians in the Reformed tradition.

2. The word "Reformed" refers to those churches based on the theology of the
sixteenth-century Reformer John Calvin (and to a lesser extent Ulrich Zwingli).
John Knox brought Calvin's ideas to Scotland, where the Reformed churches
became known as "Presbyterian" because of their principle of being ruled by "pres-
byters" (elders), both teaching elders (ministers) and ruling elders.

In addition, this book invites church leaders to explore what the confessions mean for the practical decisions that they will make as members of sessions and boards of deacons. How can the confessions guide ministers, elders, and deacons as they consider how to use money, minister to the dying, or celebrate baptism and the Lord's Supper? How can a session or a board of deacons learn to refer as often to the *Book of Confessions* as to the *Book of Order* to orient its work?

This book will be especially helpful to sessions as they train new leaders and provide for the continuing education of their members; to presbytery committees on preparation for ministry as they guide and instruct candidates for the ordained ministry of Word and Sacrament; to seminary students preparing for ordination examinations; to pastors, elders, and deacons when asked what Presbyterians and other Christians in the Reformed tradition believe; and indeed to anyone who simply wants to know more about Reformed belief and practice. Reformed confessions have never been meant just for Presbyterians; they represent a rich spiritual legacy that belongs to all Christians, even as members of other churches affirm the special insights of their own traditions.

The first ordination vow asks us to put our trust in Jesus Christ as Lord and Savior, the One through whom we know God as Father, Son, and Holy Spirit.[3] In the second vow, we promise to accept the Scriptures as the unique and authoritative witness to Christ. The third vow then turns to the church's confessions: "Do you receive and adopt the essential tenets of the Reformed faith as expressed in the confessions of our church as authentic and reliable expositions of what Scripture leads us to believe and do, and will you be instructed and led by those confessions as you lead the people of God?"

A good deal is packed into these words. Note, first, that we are not asked to subscribe to every word in the *Book of Confessions*, but rather to receive and adopt their "essential tenets." But just

3. For a list of the ordination vows, see the Appendix.

what are these essential tenets? Nowhere has the church listed them. While chapter 2 of the Form of Government (see G-2.0500) does state some of the "great themes" of the Reformed tradition (election, covenant, stewardship, and justice), it does not call them essential tenets. And the absence of a list is not an oversight. Rather, our Reformed tradition has understood presbyteries (in the case of ministers) and sessions (in the case of elders and deacons) to be charged to discern, in direct conversation with candidates for ordination, whether they do indeed receive and adopt what is essential in the confessions.

No checklist can do the job because one person's way of expressing the faith differs from another's. We do not always use the same language or concepts even when we believe the same things. Moreover, while some essentials continue over time (such as God as Creator, or Jesus Christ as human and divine), others seem to fall away or newly to emerge. In the early twentieth century, some Christians believed that a literal understanding of the virgin birth was an essential; others, however, regarded it as a symbolic way of pointing to the uniqueness of Christ. And today, many of us would regard a commitment to combating racism as essential to Christian faith, whereas the Reformation-era confessions say nothing about it.

A second key element of the third ordination vow is its description of the confessions as "authentic and reliable expositions of Scripture." Let us, for a moment, think about the Bible and why and how we interpret it. In Scripture, we encounter diverse materials from many different centuries of Israel's and the church's life. It is not obvious how these materials fit together or how we should make sense of apparent contradictions between one biblical affirmation and another. Moreover, the Scriptures have been and can be interpreted from many different points of view. Who is right? We will need nothing less than God's assistance if we are to read Scripture rightly.

According to the Reformed tradition, God has guided the church in composing confessions to help us do just that. They declare that Scripture is the "unique and authoritative witness" to Jesus Christ. In it we read of God's promise to Israel of a coming

Messiah; of Jesus' birth, ministry, suffering, crucifixion, resurrection, ascension, and promised return; and of the early church's experience of the living, resurrected Christ in its midst through the power of the Holy Spirit.

Finally, the third ordination vow asks church leaders to be "instructed and led" by the confessions, while the next ordination question (4) summarizes the first three and commits us to be "guided" by the confessions. "Instructed," "led," "guided": these words ask us to attend carefully, faithfully, and continually to the confessions and their teachings. As the Form of Government notes, while the confessions are "subject to the authority of Jesus Christ, the Word of God, as the Scriptures bear witness to him, . . . they are, nonetheless, standards. They are not lightly drawn up or subscribed to, nor may they be ignored or dismissed. The church is prepared to counsel with or even to discipline one ordained who seriously rejects the faith expressed in the confessions" (G-2.0200). The confessions matter, because they "guide the church in its study and interpretation of Scripture, . . . summarize the essence of Christian tradition, . . . direct the church in maintaining sound doctrine, [and] equip the church for its work of proclamation" (G-2.0100). The church promises us that if we are instructed, led, and guided by the confessions, we will know Christ more fully and will live more faithfully as his disciples.

The practical relevance of the *Book of Confessions* becomes especially evident when the Form of Government lists the church's expectations of those who serve in church office: All "who are called to office in the church are to lead a life in obedience to Scripture and in conformity to the historical confessional standards of the church" (G-6.0106b). Moreover, "it is necessary to the health and integrity of the church that the persons who serve in it as officers shall adhere to the essentials of the Reformed faith and polity as expressed in the *Book of Confessions* and the Form of Government" (G-6.0108).

The specific duties of ministers, elders, and deacons underline the importance of the *Book of Confessions* to church office. Ministers are "to commend the gospel to all persons . . . [by] studying, teaching, and preaching the Word of God" (G-6.0201b). For this reason, inquirers and candidates for the ministry of Word and Sacrament should have "familiarity with the Bible and the confessions" (G-14-0412), and they will be expected to demonstrate this familiarity on the church's ordination examinations.

Elders and deacons too should be well grounded in the confessions, because the first "duty of elders, individually and jointly, [is] to strengthen and nurture the faith and life of the congregation committed to their charge" (G-6.0304; see also G-10.0102), while deacons are responsible for "sympathy, witness, and service after the example of Jesus Christ . . . to those who are in need" (G-6.0401–2). The Form of Government charges the session to "provide for a period of study and preparation [for both elders and deacons], after which the session shall examine the officers elect as to their personal faith; knowledge of the doctrine, government, and discipline contained in the Constitution of the church; and the duties of the office" (G-14.0240). Because the *Book of Confessions* is part 1 of the church's Constitution, it is an essential part of this training.

The Form of Government further prescribes that, once constituted, the session is to "engage in a process for education and mutual growth of [its] members" (G-10.0102k). Continuing education that includes the *Book of Confessions* and its theological foundations will help pastors and elders grow in faith, so that they are better able to articulate what the church believes and to invite others into new life in Christ (see G.10-0102a). Continuing study of the confessions is of equal importance for deacons.

The ordination vows suggest that every church leader should have a copy of the Bible, the *Book of Confessions*, and the *Book of Order* on their nightstand or a nearby reference shelf. They are the church's foundational resources for pointing us to Christ and guiding our believing and doing. They summarize what Presbyterians believe.

The guidebook that you presently have in hand has neither their authority nor their wisdom, but if it helps you open the *Book of Confessions* more often and understand its teachings more fully, it will have succeeded in its purpose.

FOR DISCUSSION

Concerns Raised in the Opening Dialogue

Am I ready to serve as an ordained church leader?
Understanding the confessions seems like an awfully tall order.
The language of the confessions is sometimes dated and difficult.
Are the confessions really relevant to the work that we will do
  as church leaders?

Questions

1. What concerns do you have as you consider your call to
   serve as a church officer (minister, elder, or deacon)?
2. Have you ever encountered the *Book of Confessions* before?
   What are your impressions of it?
3. Why do you think the church asks you to be led, instructed,
   and guided by the confessions?
4. How do you think they might strengthen your service as a
   church leader?

CHAPTER 1

WHY DO WE HAVE CONFESSIONS, AND WHAT ARE THEY?

Opening Prayer: Holy God, teach us to confess you as the Father Almighty, Maker of heaven and earth; the Lord Jesus Christ, who is God of God and Light of Light; and the Holy Spirit, the Lord and Giver of life. Teach us to proclaim your story of salvation, which reaches from the creation of all things visible and invisible to the resurrection of the dead and the life of the world to come. And guard us as your church that we may be one, holy, catholic, and apostolic. In Christ's name. Amen.[1]

Martha: I notice that the Constitution of the Presbyterian Church (U.S.A.) has two parts: a *Book of Confessions* (part 1) and a *Book of Order* (part 2). How do they fit together?

Jerry: That's a good question. It seems to me that the confessions should make a difference for the way we govern the church, but I have no idea how we would make practical use of them.

---

1. Based on the Nicene Creed.

Lisa: I see that the *Book of Confessions* has twelve documents representing nearly twenty centuries of Christian history. They can't all be talking about the same thing.

Max: Well, even though we have taken vows to be guided and instructed by them, I'm not even sure what a confession is.

When we hear the word "confession," we often think about the Bible's charge to us to confess our sins. But confession can also mean declaring what we believe, as we see in the opening words of the First Letter of John: "We declare to you what was from the beginning, what we have heard, what we have seen with our eyes, what we have looked at and touched with our hands, concerning the word of life" (1 John 1:1).

The church of Jesus Christ came into existence because of what the first disciples had experienced: that the Jesus who had died on the cross was now the Jesus whom God had raised from the dead. The new way of life that Jesus' followers had received from their Savior on earth had not come to an end with his death. God had been faithful still. Early Christians, therefore, could not keep quiet about what they had experienced. Like their Hebrew forebears, they searched for the right words to make witness to God's mighty acts. Jewish Christian communities declared that Jesus is the Christ (Greek for Messiah; see, for example, Mark 8:29). Gentile Christian communities proclaimed Jesus as Lord (typical for Paul, as in Rom. 10:9).

Soon other and more developed confessions of faith emerged:

> Who, though he was in the form of God, did not regard equality with God as something to be exploited, but emptied himself, taking the form of a slave, being born in human likeness. And being found in human form, he humbled himself and became obedient to the point of death—even death on a cross. Therefore God also highly exalted him. . . . (Phil. 2:6–9)

> He is the image of the invisible God, the firstborn of all creation; for in him all things in heaven and on earth were created,

things visible and invisible. . . . He himself is before all things, and in him all things hold together. He is the head of the body, the church; he is the beginning, the firstborn from the dead. . . . (Col. 1:15–18)

He was revealed in flesh, vindicated in spirit, seen by angels, proclaimed among Gentiles, believed in throughout the world, taken up in glory. (1 Tim. 3:16)

Christians further developed their confession of Jesus Christ, the Lord, as they delivered sermons, wrote letters, and composed gospels. Each of the New Testament writings is an extended reflection on what it means that the crucified One is now the risen Son of God.

The Old Testament, too, came to be understood as witnessing (in advance) to Jesus' life, death, and resurrection: "We were Pharaoh's slaves in Egypt, but the LORD brought us out of Egypt with a mighty hand. The LORD displayed before our eyes great and awesome signs and wonders" (Deut. 6:21). Now Christians had experienced the greatest wonder of all: God's raising Jesus from the dead.

Confessing the faith has five dimensions, and they characterize the documents in the *Book of Confessions*:

First, the church's confessions *grow out of* Christians' deep, inner conviction that Jesus has risen indeed from the dead. Confessing is a matter of both heart and head. When we feel "convicted," we publicly declare what we believe to be true and trustworthy.

Second, the church's confessions are an effort to *understand* our conviction that "he is risen." In the words of the great medieval theologian Anselm of Canterbury, "Faith seeks understanding." Those who confess Jesus' resurrection want to know what their faith means for every area of their lives.

Third, the church's confessions aim at *strengthening* our conviction that Christ truly lives. They offer us an anchor in times of confusion and doubt. They bind us to a truth that is larger than ourselves. People who make confession cannot easily be manipulated. They know who they are and to whom they belong.

Fourth, the church's confessions *convey* our conviction about the resurrection to the world around us. Our confession of faith can awaken faith in others. God can and does use our faith, however weak, to bring other people to faith, so that they will join in the church's confession.

Fifth, the church's confessions demand that we *commit* our very lives to what convicts us. The confessions ask us to acknowledge that we are no longer our own but rather belong to the One who has been raised from the dead and raises us to new life in the Spirit. And confessing the faith may sometimes mean sacrificing even our physical lives. Since the earliest centuries of the church's life, there have been Christian believers who were willing, if necessary, to die for their faith.

This willingness to die for God's truth has itself been a form of confession—in Greek, the word "martyr" means witness. As Ignatius of Antioch wrote so vividly in the early second century, "Come fire, cross, battling with wild beasts, wrenching of bones, mangling of limbs, crushing of my whole body, cruel tortures of the devil—only let me get to Jesus Christ!"

The *Book of Order* states that the church adopts confessions in order to declare "to its members and the world

> who and what we believe
> what it [the church] believes
> what it resolves to do." (G-2.0100)

The church's confessions are more than personal statements of faith, although individuals may claim the confessions for themselves. The documents in the *Book of Confessions* represent what we together as a church have resolved to believe and do. This kind of public, corporate confession of faith has typically taken place when the church has felt that it can no longer remain silent.

Sometimes the church has confessed its faith in response to particular crises in a confused and troubled world: The Confession of 1967 called for reconciliation in a United States riven by war, racial discrimination, and other social conflicts. The Confession of

Belhar spoke out against apartheid as practiced in South Africa until the 1990s.

At other times the church has chosen to confess its faith because of disagreements within the church itself. The Nicene Creed responded to an early church heresy that regarded Christ as less than God. The Theological Declaration of Barmen sought to clarify faithfulness to the gospel in a time in which some Christians in Germany welcomed Hitler as a new Lord and Savior.

At still other times, the church has written confessions in an effort to deepen its unity. In the sixteenth century, the Heidelberg Catechism aimed at the peaceful coexistence of Lutherans and Calvinists. A Brief Statement of Faith gave expression to the reunion of northern and southern Presbyterians in 1983. And some confessions have resulted from the church's efforts to state more systematically and comprehensively what it believes, as in the case of the Westminster Confession of Faith and its two catechisms.

While each confessional document comes out of a specific situation in the past, the church has adopted these confessions for the present. Just how does that work? On the one hand, it would be a mistake to see the church's historic confessions as divinely revealed truths set in stone, never to be supplemented or revised. Reformed Christians have always been open to amending their confessions or writing new ones when circumstances arise that call for clarifying what we resolve to believe or do. On the other hand, the church's confessions are not merely curious artifacts from a remote, ancient world. They are not dead museum pieces, only of interest to enthusiasts of history.

The ordination vows to accept and receive the confessions' essential tenets and to be instructed, led, and guided by the confessions suggest that the confessions are distillations of the church's best wisdom from over the centuries. The confessions are not equivalent in authority to Scripture, but they do have key insights that help us read the Bible as the authoritative witness to Jesus Christ. The confessions are provisional and limited expressions of faith from past times and places, yet they have unique value for us in the present, precisely because they help us see beyond our own time and place.

We might regard the confessions as beloved grandparents or elderly friends. Our elders cannot live our lives for us. Often they are unfamiliar with the social forces that have shaped us as a younger generation. Elderly people sometimes seem old-fashioned and part of a passing age. But wise elders have insights about living and growing older that we do not yet have. Their life experience offers us points of view that we might never discover on our own. Perhaps more than ever the church needs that kind of wisdom today. In an era of rapid social and technological changes, Christians often struggle to know what the church should be and do. We long for a compelling vision of Christian faith and life. We want to be able to say more clearly what is so special about our faith. The confessions can help us see our way ahead.

For most of its history in North America, the Presbyterian Church was guided by the Westminster Standards of the seventeenth century—the Confession of Faith, the Larger Catechism, and the Shorter Catechism. Whenever the church arrived at new confessional insight, it amended the Confession of Faith. In the late 1950s, the United Presbyterian Church formed a committee to propose additional revisions. The committee soon concluded, however, that the church needed a new confession of faith, in addition to the historical legacy represented by Westminster. The result was the Confession of 1967 and the creation of a *Book of Confessions* that united documents from early Christianity, the Reformation, Westminster, and the twentieth century.

The idea of a *Book of Confessions* was not entirely new. Early Reformation churches had sometimes adopted several confessional statements. Nevertheless, for North American Presbyterians, having a *Book of Confessions*, rather than just the Westminster documents, raised new questions. Were newer confessions more authoritative than older ones? Or vice versa? How should the church resolve differences or even contradictions among the confessions?[2]

2. For a discussion of these issues, see the "Confessional Nature of the Church Report" (1997), which now appears as a preface to the *Book of Confessions*.

Even today, the Presbyterian Church (U.S.A.) is still feeling its way into how to use the *Book of Confessions*. Many church leaders, even pastors, do not know these documents well or how to put them together as a whole. When the church had only the Westminster Standards, the church's key teachings seemed clear. But what are the key teachings or "essential tenets" of twelve documents that come from such different times and places?

Nevertheless, there is wisdom in having a *Book of Confessions*. For one thing, the *Book of Confessions* represents the full sweep of historical insights that have shaped our church. And for another, despite their diversity of time and place, these documents are remarkably consistent in what they teach. Their differences are minor compared to what they affirm in common. It is these commonalities—these shared, core affirmations of what the church believes and resolves to do—that we will explore in this book. We will think of the *Book of Confessions* as a good teacher who welcomes various points of view but then draws them together into a coherent vision of who God is and therefore of who we are.

When the *Book of Confessions* was adopted in 1967, it included the Nicene Creed, the Apostles' Creed, the Scots Confession, the Heidelberg Catechism, the Second Helvetic Confession, the Westminster Confession of Faith, the Shorter Catechism, the Theological Declaration of Barmen, and the Confession of 1967. At the time of reunion, the Larger Catechism, which had been one of the standards of the (southern) Presbyterian Church in the U.S., was added, and a new confession (A Brief Statement of Faith) was commissioned. In 2016, the church adopted the Confession of Belhar, after narrowly rejecting it four years earlier.

The *Book of Confessions* opens with two short, succinct statements of belief (known as creeds) that have been a part of worship for large parts of the Christian world since the early centuries: the Nicene Creed and the Apostles' Creed. The Nicene Creed was composed in the fourth century in response to an influential Christian thinker, Arius, who regarded Jesus Christ, the Son, as the highest of all creatures but less than God. First drafted by the Council of Nicaea in 325 and then completed by a second council in Constantinople in

381, the Nicene Creed makes clear that the Father and the Son are two persons but one substance. Jesus Christ is nothing less than "God from God, Light from Light, true God from true God, begotten not made, of one Being with the Father" (NC 1.2)

The Nicene Creed is the most universal of the church's confessions, since it is accepted by Orthodox, Catholic, and many Protestant bodies. Historically, it has been used in conjunction with celebration of the Lord's Supper, as the Presbyterian *Book of Common Worship* also recommends. In 1991, the Presbyterian Church (U.S.A.) adopted an inclusive language translation.

The roots of the Apostles' Creed lie in the answers that adult converts gave as they received Christian baptism in the church's first centuries. Over time, these declarations of belief about Father, Son, and Holy Spirit were developed further, until in the eighth century the Western church adopted a standard version. Among Catholics and many Protestants today, the Apostles' Creed is the best-known of the church's ancient confessions, but it is not used by Orthodox Churches. Because of the creed's association with baptism, the *Book of Common Worship* recommends reciting it whenever a baptism or a reaffirmation of the baptismal covenant is celebrated.

Like the Nicene Creed, the Apostles' Creed has a Trinitarian structure, with individual sections devoted to the Father, the Son, and the Holy Spirit. Both creeds are also structured to relate the entire biblical story of salvation, beginning with the creation, moving to the coming of Christ, and concluding with the life of the church and the hope for the resurrection and the world to come.

The next set of documents in the *Book of Confessions*—the Scots Confession, the Heidelberg Catechism, and the Second Helvetic Confession—belong to the Protestant Reformation of the sixteenth century. Each of these confessions is expansive and comprehensive, laying out the major doctrines of the Christian faith, roughly in the Trinitarian order of the ancient creeds.

Interestingly, the *Book of Confessions* does not include a confessional document directly from the hand of John Calvin (such as the Geneva Catechism or the French Confession), but one of Calvin's close disciples, John Knox, was a principal author of the Scots

Confession. Composed after a protracted period of conflict between Scottish leaders and Britain's Catholic monarchs, the confession's opening words reflect the forceful confidence of the new Protestant church (or, in the language of the Scots Confession, "the Kirk"): "We confess and acknowledge one God alone, to whom alone we must cleave, whom alone we must serve, whom only we must worship, and in whom alone we put our trust" (SC 3.01).

The circumstances of the Heidelberg Catechism were quite different. The new Protestant movement, despite its core affirmations of "grace alone, faith alone, and Scripture alone," soon split into rival groups. To Calvin's deep regret, he could not overcome disagreement with followers of Martin Luther or Ulrich Zwingli about the nature of the Lord's Supper. The Heidelberg Catechism, written soon after Calvin's death, represented an effort to bring peace between Calvinists and Lutherans in an area of western Germany known as the Palatinate.

Catechisms had developed in medieval Catholicism as a way to teach the faith with questions and answers. The Heidelberg Catechism uses this format to explicate the three major catechetical documents of Western Christianity: the Apostles' Creed, the Ten Commandments, and the Lord's Prayer. The catechism is divided into fifty-two sections; ministers traditionally preached on one section each Sunday afternoon over the course of a year.

In contrast to the Scots Confession, the Heidelberg Catechism is irenic in tone, as evident in its famous opening words: "Question: What is your only comfort, in life and in death? Answer: That I belong — soul and body, in life and in death — not to myself but to my faithful Savior, Jesus Christ" (HC 4.01). Historically, the Heidelberg Catechism became especially important to Dutch Calvinist churches, but its evangelical warmth has made it a favorite of many other Reformed believers as well. In 2014, the Presbyterian Church (U.S.A.) adopted a revised translation.

The third Reformation-era document, the Second Helvetic Confession, also has a personal, irenic tone. Written by the Reformer Heinrich Bullinger, successor to Zwingli in Zurich, Switzerland, the Second Helvetic Confession was a personal favorite of Professor Edward Dowey, who moderated the committee that prepared the Confession of 1967 and the *Book of Confessions*. The Second Helvetic Confession is especially noteworthy for its attention to matters of Christian life and ministry, including decoration of sanctuaries, singing, fasting, visiting the sick, and burying the dead. Nevertheless, this confession, the longest document in the *Book of Confessions*, remains the least known of all of them.

The Westminster Standards of the seventeenth century follow. Until the revision of ordination questions at the time of the adoption of the *Book of Confessions*, Presbyterian candidates for ministry were asked "to sincerely receive and adopt [the Westminster Confession of Faith] as containing the *system* of doctrine taught in the holy Scriptures" (my italics). The Confession of Faith indeed takes the central teachings of the Reformation-era confessions and explicates them in a logical, systematic way.

Prepared by the Westminster Assembly of Divines in England in the 1640s, the Confession of Faith became *the* confession of the Scottish Presbyterian Church and then the new Presbyterian churches in America. The Confession of Faith was amended in 1788 to reflect the separation of church and state in the new nation. Other major modifications came in 1903, when the Cumberland Presbyterian Church and the Presbyterian Church in the U.S.A. reunited.

The Cumberland Presbyterians had broken off from the larger Presbyterian body in the early nineteenth century under the influence of the Second Great Awakening. The evangelistic campaigns of the American frontier (such as in Kentucky) asked people to make a personal decision for Christ. This emphasis on human agency seemed to contradict Westminster's teaching about predestination, the idea that God alone has determined from eternity who will or will not be saved. The amendments of 1903 clarify that the church's confession of predestination must be held in harmony with human freedom and Christian missions. The Presbyterian Church in the U.S. (Southern Presbyterian Church) adopted the same changes in 1942 but inserted them in a different place. In the 1950s, the Presbyterian Church in the U.S.A. modified Westminster's teachings about divorce and remarriage, and again the Presbyterian Church in the U.S. followed suit, though with somewhat different language.

The end result was two slightly different versions of the Confession of Faith. When the northern and southern denominations reunited, the new church did not try to harmonize these differences. Rather, it laid out the Confession of Faith with separate columns for the Presbyterian Church in the U.S. and the United Presbyterian Church in the U.S.A. wherever their versions differed.

The Westminster Shorter Catechism was long popular for teaching children basic Christian doctrine. The Westminster Assembly prepared the Larger Catechism to guide preachers in presenting the church's beliefs. Both catechisms give extended attention to the Ten Commandments as a guide to the Christian life.

The last part of the *Book of Confessions* is composed of twentieth-century documents: the Theological Declaration of Barmen, the Confession of 1967, the Confession of Belhar, and A Brief Statement of Faith. None of these aims at being as comprehensive or systematic as the sixteenth- and seventeenth-century documents. Rather, the twentieth-century confessions accept the doctrinal foundations of the earlier statements while speaking to specific challenges of the contemporary world.

The Theological Declaration of Barmen was prepared in 1934 at a synod of the Confessing Church, that part of the German Evangelical (that is, Lutheran and Reformed) Church that resisted Hitler's efforts to control it. The Declaration speaks out against another church group known as the German Christians, which sought to merge Christianity with Hitler's Aryan ideology about German superiority. The great Swiss theologian Karl Barth was a principal author of this confession, and it reflects some of his key ideas, such as grounding all theology in the biblical witness to God's self-revelation in Jesus Christ. The Declaration is organized into six theses, each of which opens with scriptural references and concludes with a rejection of false teaching.

The other three twentieth-century confessions also reflect the influence of Barthian theology. The Confession of 1967 discusses Christ's reconciling work before turning to the work of the Father and of the Holy Spirit. The Confession of 1967 then focuses on the need for the church to work for reconciliation in response to racial discrimination, international conflict, poverty, and the confusion about sexuality that characterizes modern societies.

The Confession of Belhar is named after the town in which it was drafted by leaders of the Dutch Reformed Mission Church in 1982. Like the Confession of 1967, the Confession of Belhar emphasizes Christ's reconciling work and applies it specifically to the church, which is called to overcome racial prejudice and difference in its own life and the world. And similar to the Theological Declaration of Barmen, each section of the Confession of Belhar states both what the church believes and what it rejects. The version in the *Book of Confessions* uses inclusive language.

Like the Confession of 1967, A Brief Statement of Faith, adopted in 1991, discusses the person and work of Christ before moving to God (the One whom Jesus called Father [BSF #28]) and the Holy Spirit. Although longer than the ancient creeds, the Brief Statement as a whole, or significant portions of it, is short and simple enough to be recited in worship. The document lifts up the equality of men and women (both of whom are called "to all ministries of the church"), "voices of people long silenced," and "the planet entrusted to our care" (BSF ##64, 70, and 38).[3]

All who become members of the Presbyterian Church (U.S.A.) are asked to confess that "Jesus Christ is my Lord and Savior." People called to ordained offices take additional vows that build on this foundation. As we have seen, we promise to "accept the Scriptures of the Old and New Testaments to be, by the Holy Spirit, the unique and authoritative witness to Jesus Christ in the Church" and to "receive and adopt the essential tenets of the Reformed faith as expressed in the confessions of our church as

3. For further information about the historical context and key teachings of each confession, see the brief introductions in the *Book of Confessions*. Other helpful resources include the following: Jack Rogers, *Presbyterian Creeds: An Introduction to the Book of Confessions* (Louisville, KY: Westminster John Knox Press, 1991); Joseph D. Small, ed., *Conversations with the Confessions* (Louisville, KY: Geneva Press, 2005); and *Book of Confessions: Study Edition* (Louisville, KY: Geneva Press, 1999), rev. ed. (Louisville, KY: Westminster John Knox, 2017). For a more scholarly treatment, see Jan Rohls, *Reformed Confessions: Theology from Zurich to Barmen* (Louisville, KY: Westminster John Knox Press, 1998).

authentic and reliable expositions of what Scripture leads us to believe and do."

The confessions are the corporate wisdom of the church from over the centuries. We turn to them in the conviction that we are more apt to come to God's truth when we struggle together with others to read the Scriptures in order to know Jesus Christ. We look to the wider communion of saints for help—both those around us here and now and those who have gone on ahead of us. Our wise grandparents and elders now speak to us through the confessions.

FOR DISCUSSION

Concerns Raised in the Opening Dialogue

How do the *Book of Confessions* and the *Book of Order* fit together?

How can church leaders make use of the *Book of Confessions* for practical decision making?

The confessions come from such different times and places that they can't all be talking about the same thing.

What is a confession?

Questions

1. Have you ever tried to write a personal confession of faith? What would you include in it?
2. Which, if any, of the confessions are you already familiar with? Are there any that have a special meaning for you?
3. Who has been a wise elder for your personal walk in faith?
4. Why do you think confessions are important for the life of the church?

CHAPTER 2

LEARNING TO LISTEN
FOR GOD'S WORD

Opening Prayer: Lord, may the Scriptures focus us again on what you have already done and what you are still doing for us. May they direct us especially to your Son Jesus Christ, who was born, suffered, was crucified and buried; who rose from the dead and ascended into heaven; and who sits on your right hand and will come again. We thank you for all of your promises of communion, forgiveness, resurrection, and life everlasting in him. Amen.[1]

Martha: I must admit that I feel a bit guilty. I think that I should read the Bible more than I really do—and I suspect that many of our fellow church members feel the same way.

Jerry: It seems to me that church leaders should set a good example for the rest of the congregation. Could we make Bible study a regular part of our meetings?

Lisa: That makes me uneasy. I've never taken any classes on the Bible, and when I try to read it on my own, I sometimes feel lost.

---

1. Based on the Apostles' Creed.

Max: I know what you are saying, and yet Scripture has sometimes spoken to me about God's love in a way that no other words can. I listen for that in every sermon and Bible study.

In the midst of life's many demands and opportunities, human beings have a deep desire to know what really matters. We long for guidance. Not that anyone else can finally decide for us, but we know that we are not smart enough to figure out everything on our own. We need wisdom from beyond ourselves.

Another way to put the matter is this: What should be authoritative for my life? I am not talking about authoritarianism, where someone else imposes their will on mine. Rather, I am asking about what I can believe in, what I can trust. Today many voices want us to listen to them: advertisers, politicians, teachers, the media, successful business leaders, and TV personalities, among others. And in resistance to them, we sometimes conclude that we can trust no one besides ourselves. But can we trust even ourselves when our own thoughts and feelings pull us first in one direction, then in another?

Christians believe God to be their ultimate authority. If we are to know what to do, we must seek the will of God. To know God and God's will, the church tells us to turn to Scripture. But, as we have noted, the Bible is a complex book, with diverse materials from vastly different times and places. Just how do we sort out God's Word from the words of the Bible's human authors or from what we ourselves wish that the Scriptures would say?

The *Book of Confessions* can help.

The point of reading the Bible is to hear what the living God is saying to us: to listen to God's Word.[2] Sometimes the confessions seem to equate Scripture and the Word of God. In the words of the Second Helvetic Confession, "We believe and confess the canonical Scriptures of the holy prophets and apostles of both Testaments to be the true Word of God. . . . [God] still speaks to us through the Holy Scriptures" (SH 5.001).

---

2. Instead of the Bible, we can also say "Scripture" or "the Scriptures."

But the Second Helvetic Confession goes on to say that preaching of the Word is also the Word of God, and that no "other Word of God is to be invented [or] is to be expected from heaven" (SH 5.004). Those who preach bear special responsibility to help us hear what God is saying to us today.

The twentieth-century confessions define the Word of God from yet another angle. The Theological Declaration of Barmen tells us that "Jesus Christ, as he is attested for us in Holy Scripture, is the one Word of God which we have to hear and which we have to trust and obey in life and in death" (DB 8.11, echoing the first question of the Heidelberg Catechism). The Confession of 1967 declares that "the one sufficient revelation of God is Jesus Christ, the Word of God incarnate, to whom the Holy Spirit bears unique and authoritative witness through the Holy Scriptures, which are received and obeyed as the Word of God written" (C67 9.27).

Taken as a whole, then, the confessions support an idea of the Reformed theologian Karl Barth, that the Word of God has three forms: Christ the Word, the written Word of Scripture, and the preached Word. Scripture is authoritative when it is interpreted, especially through the church's preaching, so as to point us to the risen Jesus.

What about other kinds of authority? How do they relate to the biblical witness? Can we reason our way to God by looking at the order of creation? What about the Roman Catholic position that the gospel has been handed down through both Scripture and ancient church traditions, such as the veneration of Mary? And many Christians regard personal experience as a means by which God may speak to us, perhaps as we pray or feel the Holy Spirit at work in us or in events around us.

The confessions do not deny that revelation can take place in many different ways. But the confessions insist that Scripture is uniquely reliable, authoritative, and complete. As the Westminster Larger Catechism teaches, "The very light of nature in man, and the works of God, declare plainly that there is a God; but his Word and Spirit only, do sufficiently and effectually reveal him unto men for their salvation" (WLC 7.112; see also WC 6.001).

Similarly, the Westminster Confession of Faith declares that "all things necessary for . . . man's salvation, faith, and life [are] either expressly set down in Scripture, or . . . may be deduced from [it]." Therefore, we do not need "new revelations of the Spirit, or traditions of men" (WC 6.006; see also SH 5.013–14).

In the twentieth century, the German Christian supporters of Hitler believed that God had revealed his will in the rise of a proud, new Germany under Nazi leadership. Nazi torchlight parades with thousands of goose-stepping soldiers created a mystical drama that seemed to bring God closer to the German people. But the Theological Declaration of Barmen rejects the false doctrine "that the Church could and would have to acknowledge as a source of its proclamation, apart from and besides this one Word of God, still other events and powers, figures and truths, as God's revelation" (DB 8.12). Only Scripture in its witness to Jesus Christ can reveal God's will to us.

But just what does Scripture teach us about Christ? After all, a person can interpret the Bible from many different angles: as a great literary classic that has influenced Western literature, including Dante, Shakespeare, Mark Twain, and many others; as the history of the ancient Jewish people and the early Christian church; as foundational legends and symbols of the Jewish and Christian religions; as wise aphorisms and sayings that provide practical guidance to all people for how to live; or as principles of belief and practice that church authorities delineate and enforce.

While the Scriptures have interesting things to say about all of these matters, the Holy Spirit guides Christians to read the Scriptures for a different reason: to know God's saving ways with humanity:

> We affirm that in [Scripture] all things necessary to be believed for the salvation of man are sufficiently expressed. (SC 3.18)

> In this Holy Scripture, the universal Church of Christ has also the most complete exposition of all that pertains to a saving faith, and also to the framing of a life acceptable to God. (SH 5.002)

[Scripture offers us] the whole counsel of God, concerning all things necessary for his own glory, [and] man's salvation, faith, and life. (WC 6.006)

[In Scripture, the church] hears the Word of God, . . . by which its faith and obedience are nourished and regulated. (C67 9.27)

[The Spirit] rules our faith and life in Christ through Scripture. (BSF #60)

These statements remind us that salvation in Christ has two key dimensions: on the one hand, matters of faith, belief, and doctrine; on the other, matters of life, duty, and obedience. Salvation has to do both with what we hold to be true and with how we live it out. Indeed, what we believe shapes what we do—or, in the words of the historic Preliminary Principles at the beginning of the *Book of Order*, "truth is in order to goodness" (G-1.0304).

These two concerns, faith and life, determine the structure of several confessions. The Heidelberg Catechism has three parts: "Misery" (qq. 3–11), "Deliverance" (qq. 12–85), and "Gratitude" (qq. 86–129). The first two parts treat what we believe about God's salvation of sinful people; the third part looks at the practical implications: We have been saved "so that with our whole lives we may show that we are thankful to God for his benefits, so that he may be praised through us" (HC 4.086).

The Westminster Larger Catechism has two major divisions: first, "what man ought to believe concerning God" (qq. 6–90), and second, "having seen what the Scriptures principally teach us to believe concerning God, . . . what they require as the duty of man" (qq. 91–196). The Westminster Shorter Catechism has a similar structure.

A similar pattern appears in some of the twentieth-century confessions. The Confession of 1967 discusses "God's work of salvation" (C67 9.08–30) before moving to "the [church's] ministry of reconciliation" (C67 9.31–52). A Brief Statement of Faith establishes that what we believe about God (BSF ##1–57) leads to our living rightly in the church and the world (BSF ##58–76).

As noted earlier, the twentieth-century confessions emphasize that the Scriptures not only inform us about salvation but also point us to the Savior, the risen Christ, in our midst. The Bible is more than a textbook or reference work. It confronts us with the living Jesus Christ, who is "God's assurance of the forgiveness of all our sins, and . . . also God's mighty claim upon our whole life" (DB 8.14).

From its beginnings, the church has had to clarify which Jewish and Christian writings belong to Scripture, "the canon" (the church's authoritative writings). Should Christians retain the books of the people of Israel or just read the works of Christ's apostles? What should we do with those writings that appear in the ancient Greek version of the Old Testament (the Apocrypha), but not in the Hebrew version of the Bible? Which of the many early Christian writings point reliably to Christ as the risen Lord and Savior? Or, in the words of the Nicene Creed, in which writings has the Holy Spirit truly "spoken" (NC 1.3)?

These questions were sharply debated again at the time of the Reformation. The Scots Confession asserts that "the doctrine taught in our Kirks [is] contained in the Old and New Testaments, in those books which were originally reckoned canonical" (SC 3.18), an allusion to the church father Jerome, who in the fourth century translated the Hebrew version of the Old Testament (without the Apocrypha) into Latin (the Vulgate translation).

A century after the Reformation began, the Westminster Confession of Faith was even more explicit. After establishing the authority of Scripture in its opening article, the Confession of Faith, uniquely among the confessions, provides a list of authoritative biblical books (WC 6.002). The apocryphal writings are not included. Further, Westminster argues that the Apocrypha is neither divinely inspired nor of special value to Christians (WC 6.003).

The judgment of the Second Helvetic Confession is only slightly less harsh. The confession acknowledges that the apocryphal writings have traditionally been read in the churches but declares that they are not "an authority from which the faith is to be established" (SH 5.009).

Some Christian traditions (Roman Catholic and Eastern Orthodox) have retained the Apocrypha as part of their canon. Others (such as the Anglican tradition) provide for the reading of the Apocrypha in worship but regard it as less authoritative than the canonical books of the Old and New Testaments. Protestants in the Reformed tradition, however, do not regard the apocryphal writings as part of their Bible and do not use it in worship.

The confessions declare that the unique capacity of the canonical Scriptures to point us to Christ comes directly from God, not from any other source. Here the confessions differentiate themselves from two other possibilities. On the one hand, some Christian traditions, such as the Roman Catholic, have emphasized the authority of the church. Because God has uniquely endowed the church with the Holy Spirit, the Scriptures have authority only insofar as the church gives them authority. The church stands above the Scriptures. Taken to an extreme, this position asserts that individual church members do not even need to read the Bible. Church authorities will tell people what the Bible asks them to believe and do.

On the other hand, some Protestants have claimed that the Bible establishes its own authority. A person should be able to pick up the Bible on their own and be persuaded by "the heavenliness of the matter, . . . the majesty of the style, . . . [and] the many other incomparable excellencies" (as WC 6.005 describes this position). For representatives of this approach, if people would just pick up the Bible and read it, it would persuade them of God's truth. We do not need any special help to interpret Scripture rightly; our own reason and experience suffice.

The confessions reject both of these positions. The confessions argue that the power of the Scriptures to point us to Christ depends ultimately on God's Holy Spirit, not on the church or the literary qualities of the Scriptures themselves: "We affirm and avow their authority to be from God and not . . . men or angels" (SC 3.19; see also SH 5.013–14). "The Spirit of God, bearing witness by and with the Scriptures in the heart of man, is alone able fully to persuade it that they are the very word of God" (WLC 7.114).

This conjoining of Scripture and the Holy Spirit has implications not only for establishing the authority of Scripture but also for how we go about interpreting the Bible. The confessions are convinced that we need the Spirit's help if we are to read Scripture as the unique and authoritative witness to Jesus Christ.

> The interpretation of Scripture . . . pertains to the Spirit of God by whom the Scriptures were written. (SC 3.18)

> We acknowledge the inward illumination of the Spirit of God to be necessary for the saving understanding of such things as are revealed in the Word. (WC 6.006)

> God's Word is spoken to his church today where the Scriptures are faithfully preached and attentively read in dependence on the illumination of the Holy Spirit. (C67 9.30)

The essential link between Scripture and Spirit also means that the Holy Spirit is never an independent source of revelation but rather will always send us back to the Scriptures to show us God and God's will. From a Reformed perspective, Christians are more than just a "people of the book." We are a people of both Word and Spirit.

This principle of both Word and Spirit lies behind the Reformed practice of a prayer for illumination prior to the reading and preaching of Scripture in congregational worship. Because we long for the Bible to speak authoritatively to us—to show us the risen Christ in our midst—we pray for divine guidance:

> Lord, open our hearts and minds
> by the power of your Holy Spirit,
> that as the Scriptures are read
> and your Word is proclaimed
> we may hear with joy
> what you have to say to us today.[3]

3. *Book of Common Worship* (Louisville, KY: Westminster John Knox Press, 1993), 60.

The right interpretation of Scripture ultimately depends on the guidance of the Holy Spirit. And the Holy Spirit, while free to blow wherever it will, works in remarkably consistent ways. The confessions identify five basic principles of the Spirit that guide us in reading the Bible more faithfully than we can on our own:

First, *Jesus Christ* is the center of Scripture. "What Christ Jesus himself did and commanded" helps us interpret the rest of the Bible (SC 3.18). "The Bible is to be interpreted in the light of its witness to God's work of reconciliation in Christ" (C67 9.29).

Second, the Scriptures, despite their diversity and complexity, are plain about matters of *salvation*. In the words of the Westminster Confession of Faith, "Those things which are necessary to be known, believed, and observed for salvation, are so clearly propounded . . . that not only the learned, but [also] the unlearned . . . may attain unto a sufficient understanding of them" (WC 6.008). The Bible is not reserved for scholars; the Holy Spirit opens all believers to the Scriptures and their witness to Christ.

Third, the Scriptures form a *harmonious whole*, rather than a collection of disjointed snippets. The Scots Confession declares that "when controversy arises about the right understanding of any passage or sentence of Scripture, . . . we ought [to ask] . . . what the Holy Ghost uniformly speaks within the body of the Scriptures" (SC 3.18). The Westminster Confession of Faith adds, "The infallible rule of interpretation of Scripture, is the Scripture itself; when there is a question about the true and full sense of any scripture, . . . it may be searched and known by other places [in Scripture] that speak more clearly" (WC 6.009).

Fourth, the Scriptures are interpreted with the help of the *universal church*. The confessions reject private interpretations of Scripture (SC 3.18; SH 5.010). Our personal readings of Scripture should agree with the most basic beliefs and practices of the whole church from over the centuries, what the confessions call the "rule of faith and love" (SC 3.18; SH 5.010). An interpretation of the Bible that contradicts what the church's creeds and confessions declare about Christ and his love for God and the world cannot be right.

Fifth, the Scriptures must be understood within their *histori-cal and literary context*. The Second Helvetic Confession holds "that [particular] interpretation of the Scripture to be orthodox and genuine which is gleaned . . . from the nature of the language in which [the Scriptures] were written, likewise according to the cir-cumstances in which they were set down" (SH 5.010). Attention to the meaning of the original languages is especially important — and why candidates for Presbyterian ministry study both Hebrew and Greek (WC 6.008).

These five principles are as relevant today as ever, whether we study the Bible on our own, in small groups, or as entire congre-gations. All Christians are called to be Bible interpreters, but our interpretations must not be based simply on "what I want the Bible to say." We need God's Spirit to discipline our reading of Scripture.

We have examined what the confessions have to say about the authority of the Word of God. But equally important is the *way* in which the confessions speak of Scripture and its witness to Christ.

The Nicene and Apostles' Creeds have no specific article on Scripture or revelation, yet they lift up the authority of the Bible by their very organization as short summaries of biblical salvation history.

The Reformation and post-Reformation confessional docu-ments relate Scripture and revelation to the life of the church and its members. The Second Helvetic Confession and the Westmin-ster Confession of Faith place their (extensive) articles on Scrip-ture at the very beginning, as though to emphasize that everything that follows, all of church belief and practice, rests on biblical foundations.

To be sure, some Reformed theologians later took the Westmin-ster Confession of Faith to suggest that the Bible is inerrant in its original Hebrew and Greek "autographs" (manuscripts) (see WC 6.008). But, as the Shorter Westminster Catechism makes clear, the point of Scripture is not to resolve all questions of historical and scientific truth but rather to point us to life in Christ. After opening with the famous words "What is the chief end of man?

Man's chief end is to glorify God, and to enjoy him forever" (WSC 7.001), the catechism proceeds to establish that "the Word of God which is contained in the Scriptures of the Old and New Testaments is the only rule to direct us how we may glorify and enjoy him" (WSC 7.002).

The Heidelberg Catechism makes a similar point in its second question. Scripture teaches us that because God has redeemed us, we owe God lives of gratitude (HC 4.002). The Scots Confession relates Scripture to the Christian life by placing its discussion of Scripture not at the beginning but rather in its article on the church, thus emphasizing that the Bible undergirds the church's preaching, celebration of the sacraments, and disciplined life in community (SC 3.18).

The twentieth-century confessions relate Scripture and revelation to God's activity in the world. As we have seen, the Theological Declaration of Barmen views Scripture as the unique and authoritative witness to Jesus Christ, who judges all history. The Confession of 1967 and A Brief Statement of Faith discuss Scripture in their sections on the Holy Spirit and the Spirit's work in the world. The Confession of Belhar also conjoins Word and Spirit, calling them life-giving forces that have conquered sin, death, hatred, and enmity (CB 10.5).

In all of these ways, the confessions make clear that the authority of Scripture is not an abstract concept but rather a living force. If we will but listen with the Spirit's help, Scripture will shape the way we believe and live, both individually and communally as Christians.

The authority of the Bible ultimately comes down to the question of whether and how we as Christians actually attend to Scripture. Do we spend regular, disciplined time with it, seeking its witness to Jesus Christ and his saving work? Do we read and hear all of the Scriptures, rather than just our favorite parts, and get a sense of how they fit together? Do we learn from the insights of the great confessions and teachers of the church, as well as from other Christians both near to us and farther away in time and place? Do we pay attention to the literary and historical context of particular passages and books?

The confessions give us confidence that every member of the church, not just the pastor or a seminary professor, is called to be a Bible reader and interpreter. If we give time to the Scriptures, even if only for a few minutes each day, we will find authoritative guidance for our otherwise confused lives. To be sure, the Bible will not immediately resolve many of our practical problems: what vocation to pursue, whom to vote for, or what causes to give our money and energies to. But even when the Scriptures do not give us what we want, they always tell us what we ultimately need to know.

They will remind us again and again that there is a God, that this God seeks loving relationship with us, and that this God has come to us as Jesus Christ. And in a way that we can trust, even if we do not fully understand, the Bible will bring Jesus Christ into focus for us not simply as an ancient historical figure but also as a living presence. Through the words of Scripture, Christ himself somehow speaks a living Word to us: a Word of joy and admonition, comfort and call, and new life and repentance. The confessions direct us to the very core of the Savior's message to us and all men and women.

Let us, then, not lose any opportunity in our meetings, our worship, our educational programs, and our fellowship to hear the Bible's unique and authoritative witness to Jesus Christ.

FOR DISCUSSION

Concerns Raised in the Opening Dialogue

We sometimes feel guilty about not reading the Bible more.

How can church leaders make the Bible a regular part of their lives and meetings?

We are not always sure what we're looking for when we open the Bible.

How can we discover Scripture's capacity to touch us with God's love?

Questions

1. To whom or what do you turn when you need guidance for your life?
2. Do you have a regular practice of reading Scripture? If so, what helps you maintain it? If not, what makes it hard for you to establish a pattern?
3. How could the confessions help you know what to look for, when you read the Bible?
4. What are some ways in which a session or board of deacons could make Bible study a regular part of its life?

CHAPTER 3

WHAT GOD IS ASKING
US TO DO

Opening Prayer: *Lord, we confess and acknowledge thee as one God alone, to whom alone we must cleave, whom alone we must serve, whom only we must worship, and in whom alone we put our trust. Give thy servants strength to speak thy Word with boldness, and let all peoples cleave to the true knowledge of thee. In Christ's name. Amen.*[1]

Martha: We always open our meetings with prayer, asking God to guide us. But I wish that I knew better how to discern God's will.

Jerry: I think that we just have to do the best that we can. Who knows what God really wants of us? God is too mysterious.

Lisa: I worry that we make most of our decisions based on what will attract new people into our congregation or will keep the people who are already here happy. And how do we figure out what God really wants when we reach an impasse and disagree about the best way forward?

1. Based on SC 3.01 and 3.25.

Max: We believe that God is good, so it seems to me that we should do what is good for the most people in the congregation.

George Gallup, the famous pollster, has reported that the vast majority of Americans call themselves religious "believers." Nevertheless, says Gallup, God does not make a significant difference for their lives. Surveys have established that large numbers of "religious" Americans do not know the basic teachings of their faith, do not live according to its ethical guidelines, and do not regularly participate in the life of a religious community. While Americans are not "theoretical atheists," many of us are "practical atheists."

Do people today really believe in God, and if they say that they do, which "God" do they believe in? God should be the most pressing question of our time, but for many people it is not even on the radar screen. On the one hand, the successes of science seem to make God less necessary to us. With the help of medicine, technology, and good nutrition, we have acquired powers that earlier generations never could have imagined. Sick people used to have no other option than praying for miraculous healing, but now we turn to doctors.

On the other hand, even people in prosperous, modern societies sense that larger, uncontrollable powers and forces bear down upon us. War, violence, and conflict unexpectedly erupt and threaten us. Rapid changes in social values and practices throw us off balance. Overly crowded schedules, the need constantly to assert ourselves against others in a competitive world, and feelings of fragmentation and loneliness leave us discontent and even fearful. We are not sure what we can really count on, what is true and reliable.

In such a world, many humans long for harmony, community, safety, and a world beyond tragedy and ambiguity. We wonder whether there is something more than just us in the universe — whether there is perhaps an ultimate power of mercy, love, and grace that can touch us and protect us. We seek experiences of transcendence that offer us something like "God," whether in the awesome beauty of nature, music, or art, or in self-destructive ways, as when people turn to drugs or sensual pleasures to fill their inner emptiness.

What the confessions tell us about God can help us make sense of our deepest fears and longings.

The confessions declare that there is a God, and that this God asks for our ultimate trust and loyalty. The confessions are certain that there is an ultimate Being who meets us in life and death, whether we are aware of its existence or not. And when we talk about God, say the confessions, we must also speak about our-selves, because God has chosen to be God not without us but rather alongside us and for us.

Each of the documents in the *Book of Confessions* gets at this ulti-mate relationship between God and humans. The ancient creeds begin with the affirmation "I/we believe in God." We have been created, moreover, not only to believe that there is a God, but also to know this God and to turn to this God.

Both the Nicene and the Apostles' Creeds speak of God as "the Father Almighty." The word "Father" here is meant not to desig-nate God as male but rather to establish that God is the source of all that exists. Such a God deserves to be "worshipped and glori-fied" (NC 1.3). At the same time, this almighty God is not a dis-tant, nameless force. Rather, God is a personal Being, One whom we can address as trustingly as we would a loving parent, One who speaks personally to us.

The Reformation and post-Reformation confessions employ language about God and humans that is even more strongly rela-tional. The Scots Confession uses such words as "cleave," "serve," "worship," and "trust" to describe our relationship to God. More-over, as the confession declares, it is God *alone* to whom we cleave, and whom we serve and worship, and in whom we trust (SC 3.01).

Similarly, the Heidelberg Catechism emphasizes "trust" and does so in a highly personal and intimate way: "I trust God so much that I do not doubt that he will provide whatever I need for body and soul" (HC 4.026). The Second Helvetic Confession teaches that God alone is to be adored, worshiped, and invoked (SH 5.023–024). The Westminster Confession of Faith adds that all creation stands in intimate relationship to God: "To him is due from angels and men, and every other creature, whatever worship, service, or obedience he is pleased to require of them" (WC 6.012).

These ideas appear again in the twentieth-century confessions. The Confession of 1967 tells us that God "made all things to serve the purpose of his love" (C67 9.15). A Brief Statement of Faith reiterates that we "trust" in God, "whom alone we worship and serve" (BSF ##6 and 27). This God is so personal and intimate that Jesus called him "Abba, Father" (BSF #28).

The confessions are consistent in their confidence that a God exists who knows us and wants us to know him. The most basic fact about the ultimate power of the universe is that it turns to us in mercy and love.

Worship, serve, obey—what is it about the One whom Christians call God that commands this kind of trust and loyalty? The confessions carefully describe God's key characteristics or attributes.

To begin with, God is completely other. God is almighty (NC 1.1 and AC 2.1). God is pure energy—or in the words of the Nicene Creed, "light" (NC 1.2). The Reformation and post-Reformation confessions use not only biblical but also philosophical concepts to express the absolute distinction between God and his creatures (see SC 3.01; HC 4.026–027; SH 5.015; and WC 6.011).

Some of these concepts express God's otherness in terms of what God is *not*: God is infinite, immeasurable, incomprehensible, immense (beyond measure), invisible, incorporeal, and immutable. Other concepts declare what God most fully *is*: eternal, all-sufficient, omnipotent, most wise, most holy, and most free. The Westminster Shorter Catechism combines these negations and affirmations in its definition of God as "a Spirit, infinite, eternal, and unchangeable, in his being, wisdom, power, holiness, justice, goodness, and truth" (WSC 7.004). The twentieth-century confessions speak of God's otherness in more reserved language. The Confession of 1967 describes God as "majesty and mystery" (C67 9.16). A Brief Statement of Faith calls God "the Holy One of Israel" (BSF #5).

Despite God's infinite distance from humans, the confessions also declare that God is close—that the almighty One is, at the same time, a Being who comes in love to us. Even those confessions that emphasize God's distance from us declare that God also turns toward us. God is "wisdom, goodness, and justice," says the Scots Confession (SC 3.01). God is "supremely wise, kind and merciful, just and true," according to the Second Helvetic Confession (SH 5.015). The Westminster Confession of Faith—after listing everything that makes God infinitely different from his creatures—adds that he is "most loving, gracious, merciful, long-suffering, [and] abundant in goodness and truth" (WC 6.011).

The emphasis on God's closeness to us is even stronger in the twentieth-century confessions. For the Confession of 1967 (C67 9.15) and A Brief Statement of Faith (BSF #29), God is, above all, "sovereign love." The Confession of 1967 goes on to say that even though "human thought ascribes to God superlatives of power, wisdom, and goodness, . . . God reveals his love in Jesus Christ by showing power in the form of a servant, wisdom in the folly of the cross, and goodness in receiving sinful men" (C67 9.15).

But how can One who is beyond time and space enter into them? How can the God who is sheer energy, like a force field or an electrical current, also be like a person who is capable of love and kindness? What defies rational explanation about God nevertheless turns out to be true for us. The confessions capture the paradoxical character of this God in whom Christians trust and believe.

According to the confessions, the Almighty God, who seeks loving relationship with what he has created—and especially with human beings—is characterized, at the very core of his being, by relationship. God is not a nameless power. Rather, God is Trinity: Father, Son, and Holy Spirit. In the traditional language of the church and the confessions, God is both one "substance" and three "persons."

The words "substance" (*ousios*) and "person" (*hypostasis*), the Greek terminology of the early Christian church, are being used in a special way here. God is not like a material substance that we can handle and analyze. And God is not like the human persons with whom we daily interact. The word "substance" simply designates God's oneness, while the word "persons" establishes God's threeness. God is somehow both three and one, both difference and unity. God as God is somehow relational within God's very self.

God's relational, Trinitarian character can be approached from two angles. The first has to do with how we describe the relations of the three persons among one other (what theologians call the "immanent Trinity"). The ancient church councils that prepared the Nicene Creed spoke of the Son as "begotten" of the Father, whereas the Spirit "proceeds" from the Father (NC 1.2–3). The three persons, though one, are different insofar as the Father "begets," the Son is "begotten," and the Spirit "proceeds."

In the sixth century, the Western Church amended the Nicene Creed to say that the Spirit "proceeds from the Father and the Son" (the phrase "and the Son" is known as the Filioque Clause, from the Latin for "and the Son"). Since then, Western churches (Roman Catholic and Protestant alike) have included the Filioque Clause in their recitation of the Nicene Creed, as do the documents in the *Book of Confessions* (NC 1.3; SH 5.016–018; and WC 6.013). Eastern churches (such as Orthodox and Coptic), however, have not accepted it, and disagreements about the status of the Filioque Clause complicate ecumenical understanding to this day.

The second angle on God's relational, Trinitarian character has to do with the relations of each person of the Trinity to the world (what theologians call the "economic Trinity"). The documents in the *Book of Confessions* accept ancient church teaching that assigns a different role in salvation history to each of the Trinitarian persons. The Father is associated especially with creating the world; the Son, with redeeming the world from sin and death; and the Holy Spirit, with preserving the world. In the words of the Nicene Creed, God the Father is the "maker of heaven and earth" (NC 1.1), God the Son "came down from heaven" "for us and our salvation" (NC 1.2), and God the Holy Spirit is "the giver of life" (NC 1.3).

Nevertheless, all three persons participate in each of these activities. God the Father creates all things "by his co-eternal Word, and preserves them by his co-eternal Spirit" (SH 5.032; see also WC 6.022). God the Son, as the Savior Jesus Christ, "has been ordained by the Father and has been anointed with the Holy Spirit" (HC 4.031). Similarly, God the Spirit is none other than the renewing power of both the Father and the Son (see HC 4.027 and 4.045). Father, Son, and Holy Spirit are one, both among themselves and in how they relate to the world.

In sum, the doctrine of the Trinity uses paradoxical language (one and three) to point to God's otherness yet nearness. And even in his otherness, God is relational. God's very character is life in relationship.

The confessions not only establish who God is, but also tell us what God does. Two prominent themes are God the Father as creator and as provider.

The confessions declare that God is the "maker of heaven and earth, of all that is, seen and unseen" ["visible and invisible," in the older translation] (NC 1.1). God "is the alone fountain of all being, of whom, through whom, and to whom are all things" (WC 6.012). God has created the world to his own glory, and under no necessity (WC 6.012). God created it out of nothing (*ex nihilo*, in Latin) (HC 4.026) and created it good (WC 6.022 and BSF #29). But because the world is fragile and always tending toward nothingness, creation is not a onetime act but rather a continuing process. The Scots Confession says that God retains all things in their being (SC 3.01); the Second Helvetic adds that God quickens and preserves all things (SH 5.015).

The twentieth-century confessions say little about creation. What matters to them is less how God creates and more how humans respond to the creation. According to the Confession of 1967, "In its beauty and vastness, sublimity and awfulness, order and disorder, the world reflects to the eye of faith the majesty and mystery of its Creator" (C67 9.16).

Some Christians have insisted that the six days of creation described in Genesis 1 should be understood literally. But among the documents in the *Book of Confessions*, only the Westminster Standards speak of "six days" (WC 6.022; see also WSC 7.009 and WLC 7.125). And even in the case of Westminster, the doctrine of creation is important, first of all, for what it says about God and God's power and goodness, not about matters that human science investigates.

The doctrine of creation is accompanied by the doctrine of providence. The God who creates and keeps the world in existence is also guiding it. The confessions do not take the position of the Enlightenment Deists, who compared God to a person who constructs a clock and then steps away and lets it run on its own. The Christian God remains actively at work in his creation.

God is ruling the world, even if we cannot always see God's hand in specific events (SC 3.01). Nothing happens by chance (SH 5.031). The fact that God is in control of all things does not mean, however, that we should become fatalistic. As the Second Helvetic Confession states, "We disapprove of the rash statements of those who say that if all things are managed by the providence of God, then our efforts and endeavors are in vain" (SH 5.031). While God is ultimately free to realize his purposes however he pleases, God normally uses "secondary causes" (WC 6.025), that is, patterns and rhythms of nature that we can study and understand in order to protect ourselves or to harness nature's power for our good. We are not simply held hostage to random "acts of God."

The God who works through the order of nature also works through us and the decisions that we make. While we cannot know where our actions ultimately fit into the larger picture of God's directing of history, we do know that God asks us to act responsibly and in accord with his will. Even when we fail to do the good that we should, we cannot ultimately thwart God's will. The Westminster Confession argues that God permits human sin yet sets bounds to it (WC 6.027).

Christians can therefore be certain that God has "made all things to serve the purpose of his love" (C67 9.15). Moreover, we can know that God is especially concerned for his church and "disposeth all things to the good thereof" (SH 6.030). We are therefore able to live with a deep sense of trust and gratitude even in a world that often seems hostile to God's will. The Heidelberg Catechism makes an especially eloquent witness to the comfort and assurance that the doctrine of providence provides:

I trust God so much that I do not doubt
    he will . . . turn to my good
        whatever adversity he sends upon me
        in this sad world.
God is able to do this because he is an almighty God
and desires to do this because he is a faithful Father.
(HC 4.026)

[God] so rules . . . that
    leaf and blade,
    rain and drought,
    fruitful and lean years,
food and drink,
health and sickness,
prosperity and poverty —
all things, in fact,
come to us
    not by chance
but by his fatherly hand.
(HC 4.027)

[Therefore] we can be patient when things go against us,
    thankful when things go well,
and for the future we can have
good confidence in our faithful God and Father
that nothing in creation will separate us from his love.
For all creatures are so completely in God's hand
    that without his will
    they can neither move nor be moved.
(HC 4.028)

What we saw about the doctrine of revelation in chapter 2 is also true here of the doctrine of God. We learn not only from what the confessions say but also from how they say it. Each confession approaches the doctrine of God from a different angle that adds something to our understanding of the One who is beyond us yet with us.

The ancient creeds do not identify or explicate specific attributes of God, such as goodness or wisdom, omnipotence or incomprehensibility. Rather, they tell us who God is by summarizing the Scriptures' accounts of his acts as Father, Son, and Holy Spirit. This way of approaching who God is and what God does reminds us that we best come to know God by immersing ourselves in the biblical story.

The Scots Confession offers us a different insight. Unlike many of the other Reformation-era confessions, the confession opens not with a discussion of the authority of Scripture but rather with a declaration of loyalty to God as the One who shapes every aspect of our lives. From the outset, the confession calls us to believe in a God who rules over every other heavenly or worldly power. God sets us free to serve him alone. We can therefore commit ourselves to God's will, confident that it will triumph, even if lesser powers that make godlike claims on us persecute us for not giving our ultimate loyalties to them.

In the Heidelberg Catechism, the discussion of God occurs in part II, "Deliverance," where the catechism explicates the Apostles' Creed. Like the creed, the catechism does not discuss abstract attributes of God. Rather, the catechism points to God's fatherly care, especially as demonstrated in Jesus Christ: "The eternal Father of our Lord Jesus Christ . . . is my God and Father because of Christ the Son" (HC 4.026).

For the Second Helvetic Confession and the Westminster Confession, the doctrine of God is closely linked to the authority of Scripture, the article that opens both confessions. God is the One who speaks to us through the Scriptures and the church's proclamation of them (SH 5.001 and 5.004). Further, in their articles on God, both confessions begin by discussing the Trinity, thereby reminding us of the full breadth of God's work in the world.

At the same time, these two confessions do differ in emphasis. Like the Scots Confession and the Heidelberg Catechism, the Second Helvetic Confession is interested not in abstract knowledge of God but rather in practical wisdom for how we should live before God. Because God is God, we rightly offer our worship to him alone, not to idols or images or anything in the created world

(SH 5.020–023). Moreover, we come to God through Christ alone, not through the saints and their relics, as in the Roman Catholic Church (SH 5.024–029). The Westminster Confession, in contrast, develops the idea of God's "eternal decrees" that predestine some humans to everlasting life while foreordaining others to everlasting death (WC 6.016).[2] Even though the confession declares that this doctrine should comfort the elect (WC 6.021), God's inexplicable power and way of ruling seem more important than God's saving mercy.

The Confession of 1967 corrects this picture by underlining a theme prominent in the Declaration of Barmen: that we can know God only through Christ and his cross. God's power and majesty appear in his desire to make trusting, loving relationship with him possible through the reconciling work of Christ. A Brief Statement of Faith makes a similar point by organizing its statements according to a Trinitarian framework in which the article on Christ precedes the article on God.

The confessions teach us that the doctrine of God ultimately goes to the question of our ultimate loyalties and allegiances. The first question before every church leader is not how to make efficient decisions on behalf of the congregation, but rather how to be true to God. As the *Book of Order* states, the session is "to lead the congregation continually to discover what God is doing in the world" (G-10.0102j). As church leaders, we can approach our decision making with the confidence that because God is in control, God's purposes will ultimately prevail to bring good out of evil and to bring order out of chaos.

When we live with the trust that God wishes good for us and our world, we become free to examine our motivations. Are we acting out of fear? Are we more concerned about people's approval than with doing what is right? Are we trying to hold on to the past? Or, alternatively, are we shaped more by the current priorities and trends of the wider culture around us than by Scripture's witness to Christ?

2. We will look at this idea more closely in chapter 5.

Perhaps the most important question will be this: How can we as church leaders conduct our business in a way that begins with God? Besides opening with prayer, how can we spend time studying the Bible and the confessions, and especially what they tell us about Christ? We might remember that nothing we do will ever be more important than acknowledging through worship our dependence on God. In relation to every business matter before us, we might ask, How can we point ourselves and the people whom we serve to the wondrous truth that there is an ultimate power of creation that nevertheless makes itself known to us as "Father" and comes to us in Jesus Christ, who in mercy calls us back to God's ways of peace and integrity?

We easily forget God, and we easily act as though our wishes and desires are of ultimate importance. The confessions challenge us to shift our vision. They call us to turn away from ourselves to a God who is the beginning and end of all things. What ultimately matters is not getting our way, but rather pausing again in awe and adoration before the One who gives us life and promises to preserve us beyond death.

FOR DISCUSSION

Concerns Raised in the Opening Dialogue

How can we possibly discern God's will?

Is our decision making really motivated by what God wants or just by what we want?

When we disagree about God's will, how will we come to resolution?

Is what is good for the most people the same as what God wants?

Questions

1. Do I feel that God is close to me or far away? When have I felt one way or the other?

2. What is a situation in which I have found it hard to see God at work?
3. What are some of the pressures that church leaders experience from members of a congregation? What can help you remember your responsibilities to God?
4. How can a session or a board of deacons make sufficient time for prayer and study?

CHAPTER 4

CONFESSING SIN AND
RENEWING RELATIONSHIPS

Opening Prayer: *Father, comfort us with the assurance that we belong—body and soul, in life and in death—not to ourselves but to our faithful Savior, Jesus Christ, who has fully paid for all our sins with his precious blood, who has set us free from the tyranny of the devil, who watches over us in such a way that not a hair can fall from our heads without your will, and who makes everything fit his purpose for our salvation. May we be wholeheartedly willing and ready from now on to live for him. We pray in his name, Amen.*[1]

Martha: I'm very angry with you, Jerry. I asked you not to tell anyone else about my marital problems. And now the whole congregation knows!

Jerry: I didn't mean to hurt you. I just thought that other members needed to know what was going on in your life, so that they could pray for you and reach out to you. And now you're attacking me in front of everyone else.

---

1. Based on HC 4.001.

Lisa: I don't want to serve in a church where the level of interpersonal conflict is so high. It just can't be what God wants. Unless Martha and Jerry resign, I will.

Max: I know that we as Christians are supposed to be forgiving because God has already forgiven us. But I don't hear anyone even admitting that they have done something wrong.

Reinhold Niebuhr, the well-known Christian social ethicist of post-World War II America, once quipped that sin is the one Christian doctrine that is empirically verifiable. We have evidence of it everywhere. But sin is also a highly mysterious and perplexing phenomenon. If God created humans for intimate, trusting fellowship with him and with each other, how is it possible that we choose to violate it? As theologian Karl Barth asserted, sin is the "impossible possibility." We apparently have no way to explain it, no matter how much it scars our lives.

Sin is no less a reality in the church than in the world. John Calvin observed that the order of statements in the Apostles' Creed makes an important point: We confess "the forgiveness of sins" immediately after "I believe in the holy catholic Church." The church, says Calvin, is an assembly of sinners who are able to live together only because they have received God's forgiveness and offer it one to another. The church is never sinless in itself, but it does look to and share in Christ's sinless nature and his victory over sin. And so for Christians the last word is reconciliation, not sin.

Nevertheless, the dynamics of forgiveness are no less complex than those of sin. When someone has hurt us, when trust has been broken, it is not entirely clear how relationship can be restored or even whether it should be restored. It sometimes seems—in a business relationship, in a marriage, or even in a congregation—that it is better for people who have hurt each other to go their separate ways than to endure the pain of each other's presence. My ability to forgive another person seems to depend on their readiness to acknowledge their sin against me, but that person may deny that they did anything wrong. Jesus speaks of forgiving a brother or sister seventy times seven (Matt. 18:21–22), but only after telling us to confront the sinner with their fault (Matt. 18:15–20). Or is it better to forgive and forget, even if the offender never admits to their sin?

How we receive God's forgiveness is equally complex. Dietrich Bonhoeffer, the German theologian martyred by the Nazis, warned of the dangers of "cheap grace," when the church proclaims God's forgiveness but does not demand that the sinner become a disciple and change their way of life. But progress in the Christian life can be excruciatingly slow, and sometimes we even seem to backslide. Can we really trust in the church's proclamation that "in Jesus Christ, you are forgiven"? And just how do we learn to recognize and confess our sins against God? Too often we reduce sin to trivialities about external behaviors, rather than deeply examining our relationship with the One who has created and redeemed us.

The confessions teach us that we can recognize sin only if we first know who and what God created us to be. Sin harms and distorts the life that God gave us, and Christ's saving work restores it. In Christ, we become who we really are: beings created to glorify God and to delight in each other's presence.

The confessions look at what God created us to be from several angles. Most basically a person consists of a soul and a body (see SH 5.034 and WC 6.023). We are not one without the other. We are ensouled bodies and embodied souls. On the one hand, our bodies—and their physical characteristics of weight, height, race, sex, ethnicity, and so on—do not alone determine us. We are also souls that enable us to transcend, to some extent, our physical realities. On the other hand, we are not essentially abstract souls—pure minds—for which the body is a mere prison until death releases us. While our bodies do not determine everything about us, they do profoundly shape the way we experience the world. A person who is five feet and three inches tall, and a person who is six feet and eight inches tall, really do see the world differently, even though they can learn to see something from each other's point of view.

A second way in which the confessions define humans is with ancient biblical images. We are the image and likeness of God

(Gen. 1:26). Much theological blood has been shed over the meaning of these words. Are "image" and "likeness" two different things? Does "image" refer to some innate human capacity, such as rationality or empathy? Perhaps "image and likeness of God" simply mean that humans are created to be a mirror or representation of God. We are to reflect back to God and to others who God is and what God ordains.

The confessions suggest several dimensions of God's being and perfection that humans should reflect, even if in a limited way, in their own being: "wisdom, lordship, justice, free will, . . . self-consciousness, . . . [and] dignity" (SC 3.02); "righteousness and holiness" (HC 4.006; see also SH 5.036 and WC 6.023); and goodness, uprightness, and freedom (see SH 5.036). The Heidelberg Catechism, however, states with special eloquence how humans mirror God: by knowing God, loving God, living with God, and praising and glorifying God (HC 4.006).

That we have been created to reflect God means that we are relational creatures. Just as God—who is relational within his own being as Father, Son, and Holy Spirit—chooses not to live apart from human partners and the creation, humans are created to relate to God, each other, and the creation.

Because humans are created for relationship with God (see WC 6.023), they need to set aside time for prayer, worship, and consideration of God's will. For this reason, according to the Westminster Standards, God has commanded us to keep the Sabbath (see WLC 7.130).

The interpersonal relationality for which humans are created is exemplified, for the confessions, in the relationship of male and female (see WC 6.023). Older confessions emphasize that within the relationship of male and female, marriage represents the trusting intimacy that should characterize all human relationships (see SH 5.034 and WLC 7.130). Newer confessions lift up that humans are created "equally . . . male and female, of every race and people" (BSF #30).

In relation to humans and the rest of creation, older and newer confessions again reflect a shift of emphasis. The Reformation-era confessions use classical biblical language of God giving humans "dominion over the creatures" (WC 6.023). All things are "subject" to us (see SH 5.034). Even the Confession of 1967 sees the rest of the creation as serving our needs (see C67 9.17). But the Confession of 1967 adds a concern that humans care for the creation, as does A Brief Statement of Faith (see C67 9.12 and BSF ##37–38). Salvation includes restoration of the ecological harmony that God intends for the natural world that humans inhabit.

As creatures in the image and likeness of God, we should know, and correspond to, God's will. In the words of the Westminster Confession of Faith, the law of God has been "written in [our] hearts" (WC 6.023). Nevertheless, we have the freedom and power not only to obey God's will, but also to reject it. We were created to reflect and mirror God, but we choose instead to promote ourselves and our selfish interests. The "impossible possibility" somehow becomes a realized possibility.

The confessions use a variety of striking images to define sin and dramatize its severity. Sin is *conspiring* against the sovereign majesty of God (SC 3.02). We choose "distrust [and] contempt" (SH 5.037). Sin is *hating* God and neighbor (HC 4.005; see also SH 5.037). We "turn against" God and each other (C67 9.12).

Perhaps the dominant image for sin from the classical Reformed theological tradition is *disobeying* God (see HC 4.007 and WLC 7.130), as when we *transgress* God's law (SC 3.14; HC 4.010; and WC 6.036). Sin is "any want of conformity unto, or transgression of, the law of God" (WSC 7.014). It is "thoughts, words, and deeds committed against God's law" (SH 5.037), or "ignoring God's commandments" (BSF #34). For the confessions, this law is summarized in Christ's Great Commandment, to love God and neighbor, and the confessions see the Ten Commandments as further specifying the kind of love that we owe God and neighbor yet fail to offer them (see SC 3.14).

More recent confessions add three other powerful descriptors of sin. It is *claiming mastery* of our own lives (C67 9.12), such that we live according to "self-interest" and with "hostility" toward God and others, as when one assumes that one is "guiltless before

God or morally superior to others" (C67 9.13). Sin is also *rebelling* against God and *hiding* from God (BSF #33).

All of these images point to the *breaking of relationship* that sin brings about. Sin violates our relationship with God, each other, and the creation. In the words of the Brief Statement, we "violate the image of God in others and ourselves, and accept lies as truth" (BSF ##35–36); we "exploit neighbor and nature, and threaten death to the planet" (BSF ##37–38; see also C67 9.12, we "become exploiters and despoilers of the world").

While we can describe the dynamics of sin, we cannot explain *why* we sin. We are left with mystery, even perplexity. According to the confessions, "God is not the author of sin," and he could have prevented sin, yet he allows it (SH 5.041; see also WC 6.031). Nor is Satan the cause of sin (see SH 5.044), yet Satan has "provoked" (HC 4.009) and "seduced" (WC 6.031) us. In the end, all that we can say with certainty is that humans themselves are responsible. Our disobedience is "willful" (HC 4.009). Any other questions about the origins of sin are merely "curious" and will get us nowhere (SH 5.042).

The Reformation-era confessions often refer to the fall of "our first parents" (SH 5.037 and WC 6.031), which "robbed" both them and "all their descendants" of the good with which God created them (HC 4.009; see also HC 5.037 and WSC 7.016). Setting aside the question of whether there was a historical Adam and Eve, we can understand the confessions to be making, above all, a theological point: Humans seem to be infected with sin ("original sin") even before they actively sin ("actual sin"). We are "conceived and born into a sinful condition" (HC 4.007). We have inherited an "innate corruption" (SH 5.037) that makes us "wholly inclined to all evil" and "from which do proceed all actual transgressions" (WSC 7.135). Sin is apparently unavoidable. It is "programmed" into us. And here again we encounter a perplexing mystery. We cannot help but sin, yet each of us remains personally responsible for the wrong that we do. Moreover, while all of us are equally in a state of sin, our actual sins do differ in severity (see SH 5.039).

Our sinfulness places us in a horrendous situation. The Scots Confession tells us that by virtue of sin the image of God has been "utterly defaced" in us (SC 3.03). We are now "slaves to Satan" (SC 3.03; see also SH 5.037). The Westminster Confession asserts that we have fallen from our "original righteousness and communion with God, and so became dead in sin, and wholly defiled in all the faculties and parts of soul and body" (WC 6.032). The Heidelberg Catechism says that we are "so corrupt that we are totally unable to do any good" (HC 4.008; see also WC 6.034). These various depictions of sinful human nature come close to Calvin's conception of man's "total depravity."

But this vivid, harsh language of defilement, defacement, and corruption can be misleading, and Reformed Christians have sometimes gone too far in making people feel guilty about everything that they do, as though they had no worth at all before God. A closer reading demonstrates that the confessions qualify what they mean by "depravity." Humans, despite their sin, have not lost the ability to reason and exercise their wills. As the Second Helvetic Confession quips, "After the fall . . . [man] was not entirely changed into a stone or a tree" (SH 5.043). And the confession further declares that "God in his mercy has permitted the powers of the intellect to remain, . . . [and] God commands us to cultivate our natural talents" (SH 5.046). The Confession of 1967 is even more explicit about the human capacity for goodness: In all ages, there have been "wise and virtuous men . . . [who] have sought the highest good in devotion to freedom, justice, peace, truth, and beauty" (C67 9.13).

So the point is not that humans are incapable of any good whatsoever but rather that even with our best intentions and our most concerted efforts, we consistently fall short of living in trusting relationship with our Creator and with each other. In the words of the Second Helvetic Confession, "Man's reason does not judge rightly of itself concerning divine things" (SH 5.045). The Confession of 1967 adds, "All human virtue, when seen in the light of God's love in Jesus Christ, is found to be infected by self-interest and hostility" (C67 9.13). "Total depravity" does not mean that we are worthless, helpless creatures. But it does tell us that there is no area of our lives exempt from sin's distorting power (see DB 8.15). We are not the selves God created us to be; we have lost our "humanity" (C67 9.12).

According to the confessions, God responds to our sin by punishing us both "now and in eternity" (HC 4.010; see also SC 3.03 and HC 4.011). We could also say, as did the ancient church father Augustine, that sin is its own punishment. Because sin separates us from God, we are "dead." Not only do we face physical death someday, but we also experience "spiritual" death right now (see WC 6.036), that is, "blindness of mind, a reprobate sense, strong delusions, hardness of heart, horror of conscience, and vile affections" (WLC 7.138). Employing biblical imagery, the confessions warn about other punishments that will come after a day of judgment: "everlasting separation from the comfortable presence of God, and most grievous torments in body and soul, without intermission, in hell fire forever" (WLC 7.139).

Contemporary confessions are more restrained in their language yet make the same point: sin causes and results in disruption of right relationship with God and each other. According to the Confession of 1967, "Against all those who oppose him, God expresses his love in wrath" (C67 9.14). A Brief Statement of Faith simply says that "we deserve God's condemnation" (BSF #39). Something about our lives and our world is fundamentally out of kilter, and we seem powerless to repair the damage—as we are reminded daily when we read the morning headlines about war, racial tension, environmental devastation, and tragic deaths, and when we remember the brokenness of our own lives.

The God who graciously created us to glorify him and to care for each other is nevertheless at work in an evil world. The assertion that God permits sin seems to put him on the sidelines, but the confessions declare that God nevertheless restrains sin and even turns it to good, as he did when Jacob's sons sold Joseph into slavery (see SH 5.041). God is able to "order" human sin "to his own glory" (WC 6.031). Just as the eruption of sin into a perfect world is mysterious and perplexing, so too is the manifestation of God's saving work to a sinful world. We cannot explain exactly why God has acted in the way that he has, but we do not have to. It is enough that God has called us back to him and that

God makes it possible for us to respond to his saving work with trust and thanksgiving.

For the confessions, all human history revolves around the incarnation of God in Jesus Christ. History prior to the incarnation anticipated salvation in Christ; history since then flows from his life, death, and resurrection. The confessions emphasize Christ as the unique mediator between God and humanity. We "acknowledge and embrace him as our only Mediator," declares the Scots Confession (SC 3.08). "He is our mediator," says the Heidelberg Catechism (HC 4.036). The Westminster Confession of Faith refers to Christ's "office of a Mediator" (WC 6.045). The Confession of 1967 makes the same point with its emphasis on "reconciliation": "In Jesus Christ, God was reconciling the world to himself" (C67 9.07). Christ heals what has been broken, reunites those who have been alienated from each other, and restores the possibility of intimate, trusting relationship between humans and God, and among humans.

Christ's status as the unique mediator is evident in his very constitution as God and human. From the most ancient to the most contemporary, the confessions are consistent in their affirmation of Christ as "fully human, fully God" (BSF #8). On the one hand, he is the Son of God, "[God's] eternal wisdom, the substance of his own glory" (SC 3.06). He existed "by the Father before all eternity" (SH 5.062). On the other hand, Christ takes upon himself "man's nature, with all the essential properties and common infirmities thereof; yet without sin" (WC 6.044). The words of the Scots Confession are particularly lovely: he becomes "body of our body, flesh of our flesh, and bone of our bone" (SC 3.08).

Within this common affirmation, the earliest creeds emphasize Christ's divinity, as they react to those early Christians (later designated as "heretics") who saw him as merely human or as nearly divine yet somehow less than God. The Nicene Creed is especially emphatic: the Lord Jesus Christ is "God of God, Light of Light, very God of very God" (NC 1.2). Contemporary confessions, under the influence of modern historical biblical studies, put the stress in the other direction. The Confession of 1967, while affirming that Christ "is the eternal Son of the Father," reminds us that Jesus also realized "true humanity." Moreover, he was a specific historical person: "a Palestinian Jew," who "lived among his own people and shared their needs, temptations, joys, and sorrows" (C67 9.08).

Drawing from the classical language of the early church, a number of confessions declare that Christ is "two perfect natures united and joined in one person" (SC 3.06; see also SH 5.066 and WC 6.044). In this respect, the biblical account of the virgin birth can be understood as a theological statement: Christ is born of the Holy Spirit (divine nature) and Mary (human nature) (see NC 1.2; AC 1.2; SC 3.06; HC 4.035; and SH 5.064). Each nature does what is proper to itself—God remains God, man remains man—but "by reason of the unity of the person, that which is proper to one nature is sometimes, in Scripture, attributed to . . . the other nature" (WC 6.049).

By bringing together divinity and humanity, and by virtue of his sinlessness, Christ is able to mediate between a holy God and a sinful world. His "work" is of one piece with his "person." The confessions especially emphasize Jesus' atoning—that is, reconciling—work on the cross. The English word "atonement" means literally "at-one-ment," that is, the uniting of what has been separated. Developing ideas formulated by the theologian Anselm in the twelfth century, the confessions see Christ as suffering death "in our stead" (SC 3.08). He was an "atoning [or expiatory] sacrifice" (HC 4.037; see also SH 5.076). "He took upon himself the judgment under which all men stand convicted" (C67 9.08). The Heidelberg Catechism succinctly lays out the idea that came later to be called "substitutionary atonement":

1. "According to God's righteous judgment we deserve punishment [for our sin]. . . . The claims of this justice must be paid in full, either by ourselves or by another" (HC 4.012).
2. We cannot make this payment ourselves; on the contrary, "we increase our debt every day" (HC 4.013).

3. No other creature "can bear the weight of God's eternal wrath against sin and deliver others from it" (HC 4.014).
4. We therefore need a "mediator and deliverer" who is "more powerful than all creatures" (HC 4.015).
5. This mediator must be "a true and righteous human" because "human nature, which has sinned, must pay for sin" (HC 4.016).
6. The mediator must also be "true God" because only "by the power of his divinity, [can he] bear the weight of God's wrath in his humanity and earn for us and restore to us righteousness and life" (HC 4.017).

To our ears today, this language of divine "wrath" and "punishment" seems harsh and perhaps even inconsistent with Christian faith in a loving God. But the confessions should be understood not so much as establishing a rigid, logical scheme of sin and salvation but more in the sense of pointing to mysteries that remain "beyond the reach of all theory in the depths of God's love for man" (C67 9.09). As much as we humans try to overcome the brokenness of our lives and our world, we fail. In our better moments, we may sense that only an ultimate power from beyond ourselves can make things right, yet we realize to our distress that we have no claims on it. Christ comes to us as the One who embodies the life that we should have, but he ends up dying on a cross. Despite these seeming contradictions, God is nevertheless at work, not simply removing his "wrath" and "punishment," but, more fundamentally, drawing us away from sin and toward him.

The confessions understand the resurrection as vindicating Christ's mediating, reconciling work. "By his resurrection he has overcome death, so that he might make us share in the righteousness he obtained for us by his death" (HC 4.045; see also C67 9.08). "God raised this Jesus from the dead, vindicating his sinless life, breaking the power of sin and evil, and delivering us from death to life eternal" (BSF ##23–26). The doctrine of Christ's ascension to heaven establishes that he continues to serve as "the only advocate and mediator for us" (SC 3.11; see also HC

4.049 and WC 6.046). And the church's teachings about Christ's return to judge the living and the dead point us to a new heaven and earth in which Christ's mediating work will be complete and sin and evil will be no more (see SC 3.11 and C67 9.54).

Ancient and Reformation-era confessions move quickly from the birth of Christ to his death ("who was conceived by the Holy Ghost, born of the Virgin Mary, suffered under Pontius Pilate, was crucified, dead, and buried," AC 2.2). More recent confessions, while not neglecting his death and resurrection, pay attention to the mediating, reconciling work that he accomplished through his earthly ministry. A Brief Statement of Faith uses a series of strong verbs to make the point: Jesus was "preaching, . . . teaching, . . . blessing, . . . healing, . . . binding up, . . . eating, . . . forgiving, . . . and calling" (BSF ##10–18).

When relationships have been broken, we sometimes despair about whether we can ever put them back together. A church session or board that has experienced violation of trust will struggle to find a way ahead. As Christians, we nevertheless have hope. But it will be a hope founded not on our own skillfulness as diplomats and mediators but rather on Christ's reconciling work in all of its mystery.

We may have to wait a while before we are able to receive the "impossible possibility" of new life together. But for a start, we can examine ourselves. For "if we confess our sins, he who is faithful and just will forgive us our sins and cleanse us from all unrighteousness" (1 John 1:9). A church session or board will therefore practice corporate confession of sin as a regular part of its life. Its members will again and again ask forgiveness from God and from each other. And then we will again commit ourselves to "the ministry of reconciliation; that is, in Christ God was reconciling the world to himself, not counting their trespasses against them, and entrusting the message of reconciliation to us" (2 Cor. 5:19). The way to self-transformation and corporate change is not easy, but we can be confident that Christ is at work in us and among us, the great mediator whose divine-human reconciling life and work we receive whenever we gather in prayer or partake of the Lord's Supper.

FOR DISCUSSION

Concerns Raised in the Opening Dialogue

We don't like others to blab about our problems.

How can we care for each other unless we know what is going on in each other's lives?

Moments of conflict occur in every church. How will we deal with them?

How do we learn to forgive each other, and how do we learn to confess our sins to each other?

Questions

1. As you think about the dynamics of sin in your own life, which of the confessions' definitions of sin seems most accurate to you?
2. How can a session or board of deacons deal with conflict in a Christian manner?
3. How would you deal with a person in the church who has hurt you but refuses to admit to it? What insights from the confessions could help you?
4. Why should Christians be committed to reconciliation? Where in the church or the world today could you and your fellow church leaders make a contribution to reconciliation?

CHAPTER 5

EVANGELIZING OURSELVES AND OTHERS

Opening Prayer: *Lord God, let Christ be the looking glass in whom we contemplate our salvation. Give us fellowship with him, and let us truly know that he is ours and we are his. We pray for the confidence to believe that you have inscribed our names in the Book of Life. In Jesus' name. Amen.*[1]

Martha: I think that we need to be doing more to advertise our church to the local community. People need to know about all the good things that we're doing, so that they will want to join us.

Jerry: That's great if new people want to become a part of our church family. But we should be telling them about Jesus and how they can be saved, not just about all of our activities.

Lisa: But the truth is that many of us in the congregation are still trying to figure out our relationship with God. Who are we to be telling others what they should believe?

1. Based on SH 5.060.

Max: In my opinion, our most effective form of evangelism would be our own example. If people see that we are truly a community of love and compassion, they will begin to understand who Jesus is.

The word "evangelism" sometimes stirs up strong emotions in today's church. Some Christians place evangelism at the center of the church's life. They believe that those who have heard the good news of Jesus Christ will necessarily want to share it with others. Evangelism, to their way of thinking, is a joyful privilege—as well as a serious obligation to a broken world that needs Christ's healing presence. But to other Christians, the word evangelism has negative connotations. To them, it suggests a kind of Christian triumphalism that presents Christianity as the only true faith and refuses to respect other religions and their distinctive paths to God. These people would say that we should live out our Christianity as well as we can for ourselves but not try to impose it on others.

The question of evangelism is complicated by two other factors. First, in truth, Christians themselves need a continuing evangelization. It is too simple to divide up the world into "Christians" who will go to heaven and "non-Christians" who are condemned to hell. Christians themselves are a combination of faithfulness and faithlessness. In Martin Luther's words, even after we have come to trust that Christ has made us his own, we are still both "sinner and saint." Each of us is still growing in the Christian faith. We sometimes make progress in Jesus' way of self-giving love, humility, and compassion, but at other times we fall back into self-centered, destructive patterns of behavior. Again and again we need to receive Christ's word of forgiveness and to take up our cross and follow him.

The second complication to evangelism is the Reformed doctrine of election. Reformed Christians have traditionally confessed that from before the beginning of time, God in his mystery has determined who will be saved and who will be damned: God has "predestined" some to eternal life and others to eternal death and punishment. While John Calvin did not invent this idea (it goes back at least as far as Augustine in the early fifth century, and both

Augustine and Calvin found firm biblical support for their position), it has come to be associated especially with Calvin and his followers. But a belief in predestination seems to make evangelism irrelevant. If the elect and the reprobate are already fixed in number, we can do nothing to change that.

The *Book of Confessions* records how the church has debated these questions over the course of history, but in the end these documents speak with remarkable consistency. Christians have a responsibility to proclaim Christ to the world, but they do so with humility both because of their own imperfect faith and because they recognize that how a person comes to faith is mysterious. We cannot program another person's conversion. We can only tell them what we know of Christ and life in Christ. As the apostle Paul declares, "How are [nonbelievers] to believe in one of whom they have never heard? And how are they to hear without someone to proclaim [Christ]? . . . So faith comes from what is heard, and what is heard comes through the word of Christ" (Rom. 10:14, 17).

Let us begin with the second complication to evangelism. The confessions declare that the "eternal God and Father . . . by grace alone chose us in his Son Christ Jesus before the foundation of the world was laid" (SC 3.08; see also SH 5.052 and WC 6.018). The flip side of this assertion is that other persons have been rejected by God (see SH 5.053). The Westminster Confession of Faith emphasizes that "by the decree of God, for the manifestation of his glory, some men and angels are predestinated unto everlasting life, and others are fore-ordained to everlasting death" (WC 6.016). Moreover, "these angels and men, thus predestinated and fore-ordained, are particularly and unchangeably designed; and their number is so certain and definite that it cannot be either increased or diminished" (WC 6.017). Strictly speaking, the Westminster Confession does not speak of "double predestination," although it often bears the reputation of doing so. Rather, it makes a distinction between "predestination" and "fore-ordination." The (admittedly complex) idea here is that God does not will the damnation of any human, but rather has only "permitted" humans to sin. All of us do sin and thereby bring God's foreordained judgment upon ourselves. Out of this fallen humanity, God predestines (elects) some for salvation while passing over the rest (see WC 6.020).

Such an idea strikes most of us as truly "dreadful," as Calvin himself once stated.[2] And historically the idea has indeed had unfortunate consequences. It has sometimes made believers so anxious about their salvation that they have tried to determine whether they are among the elect or not. Some seventeenth-century Puritans hoped that doing good works would offer evidence of their election—with the implication that a lack of good works suggested damnation. And the Westminster Confession of Faith, even though stating that "this high mystery of predestination is to be handled with special prudence and care" (WC 6.021), pointed in this direction when it stated that "those who have an "effectual vocation"—that is, are obedient to God's will—can be "assured of their eternal salvation" (WC 6.021).

A closer look at the confessions as a whole teaches us to be more cautious. The Second Helvetic Confession is especially emphatic that the doctrine of election should bring us comfort and hope, not anxiety: "Although God knows who are his, and here and there mention is made of the small number of elect, yet we must hope well of all, and not rashly judge any man to be a reprobate" (SH 5.055). It is not for us "curiously to inquire about these matters, but rather to endeavor . . . [to] enter into heaven by the straight way" (SH 5.056). Assuring us that Christ promises salvation to all who come to him, the confession quotes the great evangelical verse of the New Testament: "For God so loved the world that he gave his only Son, that whoever believes in him should not perish but have eternal life" (SH 5.059; John 3:16 RSV).

We best understand the doctrine of election as directing us to what God has determined to do from before eternity *in Christ*. He is "the looking glass, in whom we may contemplate our predestination. We shall have a sufficiently clear and sure testimony that we are inscribed in the Book of Life if we have fellowship with Christ,

2. John Calvin, *Institutes of the Christian Religion* 3.23.7, ed. John T. McNeill, trans. Ford Lewis Battles, Library of Christian Classics 20–21 (Philadelphia: Westminster Press, 1960).

and he is ours and we are his in true faith" (SH 5.060). The Scots Confession underlines this point by placing its article on election *after* its discussion of Christ the Mediator (see SC 3.07–08), in contrast to the Westminster Confession of Faith, which discusses God's "eternal decrees" even before its section on creation.

Other parts of the *Book of Confessions* further clarify that a focus on Christ impels evangelism and missionary work, rather than fatalism about God's inscrutable will for salvation or damnation. In 1903, the Cumberland Presbyterian Church, as it reunited with the Presbyterian Church (U.S.A), insisted on significant amendments to the Westminster Confession. A new section of the confession was titled "Of the Gospel of the Love of God and Missions." It declares that, in Jesus Christ, God "doth freely offer this salvation to all men" (WC 6.187). God "invites and commands all to embrace the offered mercy" (WC 6.188). "They who continue in impenitence and unbelief . . . perish by their own fault" (WC 6.189). "Christ hath commissioned his Church to go into all the world and to make disciples of all nations" (WC 6.190). A "declaratory statement" adds that Westminster's doctrine of election must be held in harmony with these amendments (WC 6.191–92).

Later in the twentieth century, the Confession of 1967 reaffirmed this new emphasis on evangelism and mission. This confession declares that the church is "sent into the world as [God's] reconciling community" (C67 9.31). The "gift of God in Christ is for all men. The church, therefore, is commissioned to carry the gospel to all men whatever their religion and even when they profess none" (C67 9.42). At the same time, the Confession of 1967 offers a note of humility about Christian evangelism and mission: "Repeatedly God has used the insight of non-Christians to challenge the church to renewal" (C67 9.42).

We now turn to the first factor that complicates how we think about evangelism and missionary work: the feebleness of our own faith. As the Second Helvetic Confession explains, "Since sin dwells in us, and in the regenerate the flesh struggles against the Spirit till the end of our lives, [we] do not easily accomplish in all things what [we] had planned. . . . [The] will is weak in us on account of the remnants of the old Adam and of innate human corruption remaining in us until the end of our lives" (SH 5.049). The question therefore arises: Who are we to proclaim the gospel to others when we ourselves are still struggling to live according to Christ's way? We will have difficulty persuading others to follow Christ when we ourselves fall short of the new life that God has offered us. And indeed, one of the most frequent and painful charges against Christians is that we are hypocrites. We talk about being "saved" yet are still all too "sinful."

The only response that we can make is this: Christians live by God's grace in Jesus Christ, not by their achievements as Christians. The good news in Jesus Christ is not that we are now sinless but rather that we are forgiven — and that we can trust God to continue to forgive us, despite our shortcomings and imperfections. The confessions use a special theological vocabulary to describe our situation: "justification" and "sanctification."

The word "justification" harkens back to the apostle Paul and his question about how we can come into right relationship with God. Paul declares that "all have sinned and fall short of the glory of God" (Rom. 3:23). We are unable to live rightly before God. But, adds Paul, we "are now justified by [God's] grace as a gift, through the redemption that is in Christ Jesus. . . . [God] justifies the one who has faith in Jesus" (Rom. 3:24, 26). Justification names what God has done to make our relationship right with him through Jesus' life, death, and resurrection.

The Westminster Confession of Faith succinctly expresses this point: "[God] freely justifieth . . . by pardoning [our] sins, and by accounting and accepting [our] persons as righteous" (WC 6.068). The Reformation-era confessions emphasize that this righteousness is "imputed," not "infused." "Infusion" would suggest that God has poured an entirely new and perfected nature into us, while in fact Christians continue to suffer temptation and sin. But God no longer counts our sins against us and instead "imputes" Christ's righteousness to us. When God looks at us, he sees not our sinfulness but rather Christ's "obedience and satisfaction" (WC 6.068) on our behalf. Similarly, the Second Helvetic Confession states that Christ's "righteousness and obedience are imputed to us" (SH 5.084). The Heidelberg Catechism uses a related term, "grants": "God, because of Christ's satisfaction, will no longer remember any of my sins or my sinful nature. . . . Rather, by grace God grants me the righteousness of Christ to free me forever from judgment" (HC 4.056).

According to the confessions, we receive God's justification by faith. Sometimes in the church today we hear people say, "Just believe, and you will be saved." But faith is not something that we do on our own initiative, as though the ability to trust in God's forgiveness were only a question of personal willpower. Rather, faith is something that we receive. It is God's free gift to us (WC 6.068). We cannot say why one person is able to trust in God, while another person is not. How people come to faith is finally in God's hands, not ours.

Justification is matched by sanctification. We are already justified in Christ, yet we are still on our way to a sanctified, or holy, life. God has already forgiven us, yet God is still at work in us to conform us to his will. Sanctification is a lifelong process. As the Heidelberg Catechism declares, we will "struggle against [our sinful nature] all [our] life" (HC 4.056). New life in Christ does not relieve us of the need to grow more fully into the image of Christ. If justification refers to what God has already done for us in Christ, sanctification points to what God is still doing. As the Heidelberg Catechism states, "Christ, having redeemed us by his blood [justification], is also restoring us by his Spirit into his image [sanctification]" (HC 4.086). The Westminster Confession of Faith further declares that the sanctifying Spirit of God continually supplies us strength to "grow in grace" (WC 6.077). And like justification, sanctification has implications for evangelism. The progress, however limited, that we make in the way of Christ witnesses to how Christ is at work in our lives.

Perhaps even more important than any growth in Christian love, compassion, and gentleness that we can demonstrate is the witness that we make by acknowledging just how far we still have to go. If it is by faith that we receive justification, sanctification is characterized by a process of repentance. In Scripture, the term repentance refers to "turning around"—making a fundamental shift in loyalties—from false gods to the living God, from faith-lessness to faithfulness, and from an old life of sin to a new life of grateful service to God and humanity. Because "the doctrine of repentance is joined with the Gospel" (SH 5.093), repentance entails amending one's ways and striving "for innocence and vir-tue in which conscientiously to exercise [oneself] all the rest of [one's] life" (SH 5.093). The Westminster Confession of Faith calls repentance an "evangelical grace" (WC 6.081). "Upon the apprehension of his mercy in Christ, . . . [the Christian] grieves for, and hates his sins, as to turn from them all to God" (WC 6.082). And just as faith is God's gift, so too "repentance is a sheer gift of God and not a work of our own strength" (SH 5.094).

In sum, the Christian life is characterized by the interaction between justification and sanctification, forgiveness and good works, and faith and repentance. When we as Christians declare God's reconciling work in Jesus Christ, we are speaking as much to ourselves as to the world around us. Or perhaps we could say that evangelism is as much a matter of our hearing God's Word for ourselves as it is of our offering God's Word to "nonbeliev-ers." Christian evangelism proceeds out of a deep sense of grati-tude for what God in Christ has done and continues to do for us as sinners. And we want others to know that God's promises also count for them.

Evangelism and mission get at the very nature and purpose of the church. For many centuries, Europe was Christian in the sense that most people accepted the authority of the church. They par-ticipated in the church's basic rituals—such as baptism, penance, and the Eucharist—and lived in anticipation (and perhaps fear) of a final judgment. The church's mission was simply its everyday ministry to its "members." Only as European nations colonized other parts of the world did the notion of mission to "pagans" or "nonbelievers" arise. And historians today point out that Christian missionary work sometimes became a tool of oppressive coloniza-tion rather than an invitation to freedom in the gospel.

A different sense of evangelism and mission developed on the nineteenth-century American frontier. The new Europeans settlers were Christian in name, but their move westward took them beyond the reach of the established churches. Groups such as the Methodists and the Cumberland Presbyterians quickly recognized the need to send preachers (often as circuit riders) to provide for worship, education, and moral training. This kind of evangelization called for individuals to make a personal decision for Christ rather than simply participate in church rituals.

As European and American societies became less Christian over the course of the nineteenth and twentieth centuries—in part because of intellectual challenges to traditional Christian belief from developments in philosophy and the sciences, and in part because of growing religious pluralism (Jews, Muslims, and other religious groups)—the church had to think yet again about the nature and purpose of evangelism and mission. Now proclaiming the gospel seemed to require more than words and rituals; the church would also make a witness by the way it related to a society in which Christianity was no longer the only influential religious force.

Taken as a whole, the confessions suggest three approaches to evangelism and mission. First, the Reformation-era confessions emphasize that the church makes its witness to the gospel primarily through proclamation of the Word and celebration of the sacraments, and secondarily through the exercise of church discipline. The Scots Confession calls Word, sacraments, and church discipline "the notes of the true Kirk" (SC 3.18). The Second Helvetic Confession states that ministers' principal responsibility is "to the teaching of the Gospel of Christ, and to the proper administration of the Sacraments" (SH 5.163), and especially emphasizes "the lawful and sincere preaching of the Word of God" (SH 5.134). Several confessions also speak of the "office of the keys" (a reference to Matt. 16:19) whereby the church's "preaching of the holy gospel and Christian discipline toward repentance . . . open the kingdom of heaven to believers and close it to unbelievers" (HC 4.083; see also WC 6.170). From this perspective, evangelism and mission aim at bringing people into a community that exercises discipline over them in order to protect its ministry of Word and sacrament.

The Declaration of Barmen affirms the centrality of Word and sacrament to the church's nature and purpose: "The Church's commission . . . consists in delivering the message of the free grace of God to all people in Christ's stead, and therefore in the ministry of his own Word and work through sermon and sacrament" (DB 8.26). But Barmen also suggests a second approach to evangelism and mission, stating that "as the Church of pardoned sinners, [the Church] has to testify in the midst of a sinful world, with its faith as with its obedience, with its message as with its order, that it . . . lives and wants to live solely from [Christ's] comfort and from his direction" (DB 8.17). The very way in which the church orders and organizes its life internally makes a witness to the world.

Karl Barth, the principal author of the Barmen Declaration, wanted the church to be an "alternative society," and his insight has inspired several more recent theological projects.[3] According to them, the church should exhibit a way of life based on Jesus' love, nonviolence, hospitality, and life in community that contrasts with the world's ethic of competition, violence, selfishness, and excessive individualism. Evangelism and mission, according to this approach, are not only about the words (of the gospel) that we speak to a non-Christian society, but also about demonstrating what makes Christian community distinctive from, yet potentially attractive to, the world around it.

A third approach to evangelism and mission, apparent in more recent confessions, emphasizes the church's responsibility to witness to the gospel by shaping the world's political and social structures. Like the Reformation confessions, the Confession of 1967 affirms that "Jesus Christ has given the church preaching and teaching, praise and prayer, and Baptism and the Lord's Supper as means of fulfilling its service of God among men" (C67 9.48). But for the Confession of 1967, Word and sacrament do not simply build up the church from within; they also equip it to be a community that works for reconciliation in light of "particular problems and crises" in society (C67 9.43).

3. Especially see the writings of American theologian Stanley Hauerwas, such as (with William Willimon) *Resident Aliens* (Nashville: Abingdon Press, 1989).

The Confession of Belhar highlights both the second and third approaches to evangelism and mission. On the one hand, Belhar calls on the church in South Africa to represent an alternative (second approach) to the segregation of the races. The church makes a faithful witness to Christ when it lives as "a community of believers who have been reconciled with God and with one another" (CB 10.3). On the other hand, Belhar challenges the church to witness to Christ through active political involvement (the third approach): The church must "stand by people in any form of suffering and need, . . . strive against any form of injustice, . . . [and] witness against all the powerful and privileged who selfishly seek their own interests and thus control and harm others" (CB 10.7).

The church is more than just another social organization where people enjoy each other's fellowship or participate in service projects. As Christians, we care about fellowship and service because the good news of God's love in Jesus Christ has touched our lives, and we wish to share this truth with each other and with people beyond the church. Contemporary theologians have persuasively argued that the church is truly the church only as it reaches beyond its walls and goes into the world to testify to Christ's living presence and transformative work.[4]

The approaches that we have identified, while distinct in emphasis, complement each other. The church engages in evangelism and mission in all three ways: as it proclaims the Word and celebrates the sacraments, as it shapes itself as an alternative community that practices the values of the kingdom of God, and as it involves itself in political and social issues. Each form of witness points nonbelievers to God's saving work in Jesus Christ while reminding Christians of their own need for continuing justification and sanctification.

Christian evangelism and mission are characterized both by audacious confidence and by quiet humility. We have absolute confidence that God forgives sin and calls people from ways of death into life abundant. But we are also humble because we know that

4. See David Bosch and his seminal work *Transforming Mission* (Maryknoll, NY: Orbis Books, 1991).

our witness is still tainted by self-interest and self-deception. We are still growing into the new life in Christ and therefore have no grounds for regarding ourselves as better than "nonbelievers." And we are humble also because we know that we cannot make others believe; only God can change a person's heart. Our task is nothing more—but also nothing less—than to bear witness to God's reconciling work in Jesus Christ. We offer that witness through divine worship, through the way we treat each other in the community of faith, and through our commitment to justice and peace in the world. In the end, evangelism and mission are the responsibility of every member of the church (see C67 9.35–37).

FOR DISCUSSION

Concerns Raised in the Opening Dialogue

How do we tell others about all the good things that our church is doing?

Does evangelism mean telling people about our church or about Christ?

Who are we to tell others about Jesus when we ourselves are still figuring out our relationship with him?

Evangelism is best done by example, not words.

Questions

1. How would you explain the doctrine of election to a friend in the church?
2. How does your church understand evangelism? Which of the three approaches represented in the confessions do you consider most important for your congregation to try?
3. What does it mean to share the gospel both with confidence and with humility? Why do we need both of these attitudes?
4. What does the doctrine of sanctification mean for the way we regard each other within the community of faith?

CHAPTER 6

THE GIFTS OF THE SPIRIT

Opening Prayer: Holy God, you promise to make all things new. Enlarge our hearts to receive your Holy Spirit, that we may be filled with peace and joy. Reveal to us all that you have done and continue to do for us through your Son, Jesus Christ. And give us strength and cheerfulness to seek your ways for our lives, for the church, and for the world around us. We pray in Jesus' name and in the power of his Spirit, Amen.[1]

Martha: I have heard many sermons over the years about Jesus, but not one about the Holy Spirit. Why is that?

Jerry: Friends of mine in another church claim that they have been anointed with the Holy Spirit. Their worship service is high energy, and sometimes people even speak in tongues.

Lisa: But I think that the Holy Spirit works in quiet ways. It's when I pray that I sense Jesus and his Spirit to be near.

Max: Part of our job as church leaders is to cultivate our members' spiritual gifts. For me, that means bringing our people together to make our church and our society better—more just and peaceful.

1. Based on WC 6.099.

The Christian tradition has generally been cautious about the Holy Spirit. The ancient creeds have a Trinitarian structure, but the sections on the Holy Spirit were historically the last to be developed—and in less detail. The Apostles' Creed simply states, "I believe in the Holy Ghost" (AC 2.3). Some of the Reformation confessions, such as the Second Helvetic Confession, have distinct sections for God and Christ but not for the Holy Spirit. Neither did the Westminster Confession of Faith until it was amended in 1903. Since then, however, the Holy Spirit has come more and more into its own, as reflected in the Confession of 1967 and A Brief Statement of Faith, which return to a Trinitarian structure and give sustained attention to the Holy Spirit.

This new interest in the Holy Spirit may reflect the rise of charismatic and Pentecostal movements, whose adherents speak of receiving special powers through the Holy Spirit. For them, the Holy Spirit endows believers with extraordinary abilities to speak in tongues, cast out demons, and resist forces of evil. While Christians from more traditional strands of the faith may be skeptical of such claims, we too may wonder whether the Holy Spirit can offer us an experience of the divine—and therefore something more than just an intellectual faith.

Christians confess the Holy Spirit yet have struggled to know just how to describe and recognize it. As we read in 1 John 4:1, "Do not believe every spirit, but test the spirits to see whether they are from God." What are the signs of a vital, Spirit-filled church? Does a person need special spiritual experiences in order to be a Christian? We turn to the confessions for help in recognizing the Holy Spirit and especially in understanding how the Spirit draws us into the life of the crucified and resurrected Christ and therefore also into deeper fellowship with each other as the body of Christ.

When the confessions speak of the Holy Spirit, they first establish that it is more than an impersonal tool or device that God has created to transmit his power to us. The Holy Spirit is not a cable that connects us to divine energy. On the contrary, the confessions regard the Holy Spirit as nothing less than God himself. Just as the earliest creeds of the church first established that God the

Father and God the Son are one God, they then clarified that the Holy Spirit is equal to the Father and the Son. The language of the Nicene Creed is especially emphatic about this point. Three times we repeat, "We believe in": "We believe in" God, the Father; "we believe in" Jesus Christ, the Son; and "we believe in" the Holy Spirit. The creed affirms that the Spirit "proceeds" from the Father and the Son, and that the Spirit is "worshiped and glorified" together with "the Father and the Son" (NC 1.3). Just as the Father has made all things, the Spirit is "the giver of life" (NC 1.2). And just as Jesus is Lord, so too is the Holy Spirit (NC 1.2–3).

This identification of the Holy Spirit with God means that the Spirit is not a free agent who acts apart from the Father and the Son. Rather, wherever the Spirit is active, it is drawing people more fully into the work of the Father and the Son. From the earliest centuries, the church's great theologians, such as Augustine, have regarded the Spirit as a principle of unity. The Spirit is the bond of love between the Father and the Son, and the Spirit unites believers with the Son, who is one with the Father.

As we noted in chapter 3 on God, the work of one person of the Trinity is the work of all three persons. But in human experience, we typically encounter God in one of the divine persons (Father, Son, or Holy Spirit). The confessions, building off of the biblical witness, attribute certain functions primarily to the Holy Spirit, many of which have to do with stirring believers to new awareness of God, to new faithfulness to God, and to new commitment to God's ways in the world. The Spirit as the "giver of life" is always drawing humans into truer, more authentic life in all of its dimensions—physical, emotional, social, spiritual, and eternal. This kind of life in abundance is ultimately life in Jesus Christ and his church.

The life-giving Spirit is associated first of all with the Father's creation of, and providential care for, all things, visible and invisible. The Spirit is "everywhere present" (WC 6.052 and 6.184) and "everywhere the giver and renewer of life" (BSF #53). The Spirit who breathed life into creation was also active as the Son entered into human flesh and history and became Jesus of Nazareth. The ancient creeds emphasize that Christ "was conceived by the Holy

Ghost" (AC 2.2) and became "incarnate of the Holy Spirit and the Virgin Mary" (NC 1.2).

The work of the Spirit is further focused on bringing people into communion with Christ. The Holy Spirit who once guided the authors of Scripture now assists us, so that when we read the Bible we no longer just see words on a page but rather recognize God's purposes in Jesus Christ (see NC 1.3; WC 6.184; and BSF #59). Further, the Spirit, in the language of the Reformation, makes Christ's benefits "effectual" for us. Thanks to the Spirit, what God offers us in Christ is not simply abstract information about God. Rather, Christ's saving work becomes real for us, redirecting and changing our lives.

As the Heidelberg Catechism reviews the different aspects of Christ's saving work on our behalf, "benefits" becomes a steady refrain (in what follows, the italics are my own): "How does the holy conception and birth of Christ *benefit* you? Answer: He . . . covers with his innocence and perfect holiness my sinfulness in which I was conceived" (HC 4.036). After declaring that Christ's death makes atonement for our sin, the catechism asks, "What further *benefit* do we receive from Christ's sacrifice and death on the cross? Answer: By Christ's power our old selves are crucified, put to death, and buried with him, so that . . . we may offer ourselves as a sacrifice of gratitude to him" (HC 4.043). The catechism continues, "How does Christ's resurrection *benefit* us? Answer: First, . . . he has overcome death. . . . Second, by his power we too are already raised to a new life. . . . Third, Christ's resurrection is a sure pledge to us of our blessed resurrection" (HC 4.045).

Further, asks the catechism, "How does Christ's ascension *benefit* us? Answer: First, he is our advocate in heaven. . . . Second, we have . . . a sure pledge that . . . [he] will also take us, his members, up to himself. . . . Third, he sends his Spirit to us . . . [so that] we seek not earthly things but the things above" (HC 4.049). In relation to Christ's ascension, the catechism asks, "How does this glory of Christ our head *benefit* us? Answer: [Through] his Holy Spirit he pours out gifts from heaven upon us . . . [and] defends us and keeps us safe from all enemies" (HC 4.051). And finally, "How does Christ's return 'to judge the living and the dead' comfort [we could also say, *benefit*] you? Answer: In all distress and persecution, with uplifted head, I confidently await the very judge who has already offered himself to the judgment of God in my place and removed the whole curse from me" (HC 4.052).

In a similar manner, the Westminster Shorter Catechism asks about the "benefits" of Christ's work for our lives (WSC 7.032 and 7.036), while other confessions make the same point by using the phrase "for us" (again, my italics): *"For us and for our salvation* [the Son] came down from heaven" (NC 1.2). *"For our sake* he was crucified under Pontius Pilate" (NC 1.2). "He was wounded and plagued *for our transgressions"* (SC 3.09). He "did rise again *for our justification"* (SC 3.10). He ascended "into the heavens, . . . where in our name and *for our comfort* he has received all power in heaven and earth" (SC 3.11). "Everything . . . he did and endured *for our sake"* (SH 5.076).

In sum, through the Holy Spirit believers receive the benefits of Christ's power over sin and death, making it possible for us to live lives of gratitude, trust, and service. Moreover, the Holy Spirit sustains us in this way of life. In the words of the Heidelberg Catechism, the very Spirit that "is eternal God . . . is given also to me, so that, through true faith, he makes me share in Christ and all his *benefits,* comforts me, and will remain with me forever" (HC 4.053). Similarly, the Westminster Confession declares that "to all those *for whom* Christ hath purchased redemption, he doth certainly and effectually apply and communicate the same . . . [by] *effectually* persuading them by his Spirit . . . and governing their hearts by his Word and Spirit" (WC 6.050). The 1903 additions to the Westminster Confession of Faith reaffirm that "the Holy Spirit . . . is the only efficient agent in the application of redemption" (WC 6.053 and 6.185; see also WSC 7.030).

The confessions teach us that life in the Spirit is nothing less than life in Jesus Christ, who became human for us, was crucified for us, was raised from the dead for us, ascended into heaven for us, and will return in glory for us. We can therefore say that the work of the Holy Spirit ultimately aims at our salvation. The Lord, the giver of life, is simultaneously the giver of new life in Jesus Christ. The Spirit sanctifies and renews us. The Reformation-era confessions often use the term "regeneration" (see SC 3.12). This is the Spirit's "objective work," as we might call it: making the benefits of Christ effectual for us. But we can also speak of how we actually experience these benefits, how the Spirit works in us "subjectively." What are the new feelings, emotions, attitudes, dispositions, and values that the Spirit implants in us when we are united to Christ and receive his benefits?

One key element of our new "mind in Christ" (the term that Paul uses in 1 Cor. 2:16) is "assurance"; the confessions also speak of "faith" and "trust." According to the Scots Confession, "our faith and assurance do not proceed from flesh and blood, that is to say, from natural powers within us, but are the inspiration of the Holy Ghost" (SC 3.12). The Heidelberg Catechism tells us that "Christ, by his Holy Spirit, assures me of eternal life" (HC 4.001); moreover, "true faith is not only a sure knowledge by which I hold as true all that God has revealed to us in Scripture; it is also a wholehearted trust, which the Holy Spirit creates in me by the gospel, that God has freely granted, not only to others but to me also, forgiveness of sins, eternal righteousness, and salvation" (HC 4.021) — and therefore "comfort" (HC 4.053).

A second key dimension of life in Christ is the experience of "enlightenment" or "illumination." The Holy Spirit awakens us to the truth about God and ourselves. As the Scots Confession says, "The Spirit of the Lord Jesus Christ . . . [removes] the darkness from our minds" (SC 3.12). For the Second Helvetic Confession, the preaching of the gospel "becomes effectual and living in the ears, nay more, in the hearts of believers through the illumination of the Holy Spirit" (SH 5.090). By Word and Spirit, says the Westminster Confession of Faith, God is "enlightening [our] minds, spiritually and savingly, to understand the things of God" (WC 6.064). The Holy Spirit gives us a new awareness of God and of all that God has done and is doing for us. Through the Spirit, the truth finally hits home for us.

A third aspect of our new life orientation in Christ is a "wholeheartedly [willingness] and [readiness] from now on to live for him" (HC 4.001). The Holy Spirit gives us a "joy in God through Christ and a love and delight to live according to the will of God by doing every kind of good work" (HC 4.090). The Spirit "[bows] our stubborn hearts to the obedience of [Christ's] holy will" (SC 3.12) and "brings forth such works as God has prepared for us to walk in" (SC 3.13). God renews our wills, "determining them to that which is good; and effectually drawing them to Jesus Christ; yet so as they come most freely, being made willing by his grace" (WC 6.064).[2]

Profound experiences of assurance and trust, of comprehension of the truth about our lives, and of desire to live entirely for Christ—these are gifts of the Spirit that reshape our fundamental stance toward the world around us. What a difference life in the Spirit can make. As twenty-first-century Americans, we are often driven by fear: fear of terrorist attacks, fear of powerful interest groups, and fear of the brutal social competition by which others get ahead of us and leave us behind. To be able to trust that God is directing all of history—as well as the course of our own individual lives—is indeed an immense blessing.

Similarly, the Spirit aids us when we are confused by the misinformation, exaggeration, and conflicting points of view that we get from advertisers, politicians, and the media. The truth of God and God's ways in Christ shows us the real purpose of our lives. And when everywhere around us we hear voices that tell us to live for ourselves even as they try to manipulate us to obey them, the Spirit promises us real life. By discovering that our deepest desire is to serve God and the people around us, we experience the freedom that only God's Spirit can give. Life in Christ—life in the Spirit— means to do the good that God has given us to do in our personal relationships, the church, and society.

While the social implications of the Spirit's work are never absent from Reformation-era confessions, their focus typically falls on the salvation of the individual. Representative is the

2. In chapter 7 we will say more about Christian discipleship and the character of these good works.

Westminster Confession of Faith, which links the Holy Spirit to an *ordo salutis* (order of salvation), a delineation of stages by which God brings an individual from the old life to the new:

1. "Effectual calling," by which the Spirit enables a person to embrace God's call to a new life in Christ (WC 6.065)
2. "Justification," by which the Spirit applies Christ's work to a person and brings about forgiveness of their sins (WC 6.071)
3. "Adoption," by which the Spirit enables a person "to have access to the throne of grace . . . [and] to cry, Abba" (WC 6.074)
4. "Sanctification," by which the Spirit assists a person to resist and overcome fleshly desires and to grow in holiness (WC 6.077)
5. "Saving faith," by which the Spirit enables a person to accept, receive, and rest "upon Christ alone for justification, sanctification, and eternal life" (WC 6.079)
6. "Repentance unto life," by which the Spirit enables a person to turn from their sin and to walk in God's ways (WC 6.082)
7. "Good works," by which the Spirit enables a person to show forth "the fruits and evidences of a true and lively faith" (WC 6.088)
8. "Perseverance of the saints," by which the Spirit abides in a person such that they "can neither totally nor finally fall away from the state of grace" (WC 6.094)
9. "Assurance of grace and salvation," by which the Spirit gives a person the means to know that their salvation is certain (WC 6.099)

Westminster's *ordo salutis* helpfully identifies the many dimensions of the Spirit's saving work. But delineating an order of salvation is misleading if it suggests that salvation consists of a sequence of stages in a believer's life. For most of us, the way to life in Christ is not so rigidly logical. Even theologians during and after the Reformation could label and arrange the stages differently, suggesting that there was not just one order. Perhaps the greatest deficiency of an *ordo salutis* is its exclusive focus on the individual and how he or she experiences salvation. The Spirit, as we noted earlier, does indeed touch our minds and spirits personally: we do experience assurance, illumination, and a wholehearted readiness to live for Christ. But the work of the Spirit cannot be restricted to individual transformation. Rather, the Spirit who was involved with the creation of the whole universe also acts to heal and renew the church and the world in which we live.

More recent confessions point more clearly to this all-encompassing work of the Holy Spirit. For A Brief Statement of Faith, the renewing work of the Spirit extends to the creation as a whole. In a time in which we "exploit neighbor and nature, and threaten death to the planet entrusted to our care" (BSF ##37–38), the Holy Spirit empowers us to "watch for God's new heaven and new earth" (BSF #75). Two other dimensions of the Spirit's work, however, receive fuller attention in the newer confessions — the unity of the church and Christian responsibility to society — as when the Confession of 1967 declares that "God the Holy Spirit fulfills the work of reconciliation in men. The Holy Spirit creates and renews the church as the community in which men are reconciled to God and to one another. He enables them to receive forgiveness as they forgive one another and to enjoy the peace of God as they make peace among themselves. In spite of their sin, he gives them power to become representatives of Jesus Christ and his gospel of reconciliation to all men" (C67 9.20).

First, the Spirit impels the church to practice reconciliation within its own life. The Confession of 1967 challenges the church to overcome anything in its life that privileges one race or economic class over another (C67 9.44 and 9.47). The Confession of Belhar emphasizes, further, that because the church is "the community of believers who have been reconciled with God and with one another," "unity is . . . both a gift and an obligation for the church" (CB 10.3) and the church must therefore reject any effort to base its life on "descent or any other human or social factor" (CB 10.4). Similarly, A Brief Statement of Faith declares that the Spirit "binds us together with all believers in the one body of Christ, the church" (BSF ##56–57).

Second, the Spirit impels the church to seek reconciliation in society. Because reconciliation does not overlook injustice but rather seeks to overcome it, the Confession of 1967 calls for the church to break down every form of discrimination based on race, ethnicity, national identity, economic class, or sex (C67 9.44–47). Further, the Confession of Belhar commands the church to follow the God who "brings justice to the oppressed and gives bread to the hungry" (CB 10.7), and A Brief Statement of Faith declares that "the Spirit gives us courage . . . to work with others for justice, freedom, and peace" (BSF ##67 and 71). As the Spirit guides people into new life in Christ, they participate in God's transformation of the whole world.

The confessions refer to additional dimensions of the Spirit's work, including prayer, proclamation, baptism, the Lord's Supper, and other forms of witness to Jesus Christ as Lord and Savior (see BSF ##52–76). Everywhere the Spirit renews people's lives and empowers the church's ministries. Nowhere, however, does the *Book of Confessions* discuss the special spiritual gifts, such as speaking in tongues or receiving divine prophecies, that some charismatic and Pentecostal believers claim and that, as they point out, characterized the first Pentecost (see Acts 2) and the early church (see 1 Cor. 14). What, then, are Christians in the Reformed tradition to make of this way of understanding the Holy Spirit?

Without making judgments about other Christian traditions, we can say that, for us, wherever the Holy Spirit is present, it manifests God's energizing love. Through the Holy Spirit, believers become certain of Christ's enduring love for them, and they learn to love God and all that God has created, especially our fellow human beings. The gifts of the Holy Spirit, as we understand them, always have to do with reconciliation, unity, justice, and peace — within each of us individually and within the community of faith, society, and even the creation as a whole. The Reformed tradition has emphasized how the Holy Spirit brings forth a new way of life both in individuals and in communities. We bear "the fruit of the Spirit": joy, love, patience, and peace (see Gal. 5:22–23).

Spiritual practices such as prayer, Scripture reading, and worship can deepen our commitment to, and capacity for, reconciliation and unity. And when we work at reconciliation and unity, we may find that our prayer and worship life also grow stronger because we realize just how completely we depend on God's energizing Spirit for everything that we are and do. Even when we feel discouraged, the Holy Spirit—the Lord, the giver of life—assures us of the Father's love and guides us into the fullness of life that is Jesus Christ risen from the dead. Through the Spirit, we are united to Christ and all his benefits, and we grow more and more into his image. And because we long for him to complete his promised transformation, both of us individually and of all heaven and earth, we boldly pray in the power of the Spirit, "Come, Lord Jesus!" (Rev. 22:20; see also BSF #76).

FOR DISCUSSION

Concerns Raised in the Opening Dialogue

Why do Presbyterian ministers rarely preach about the Holy Spirit?

Some Christians claim that the Holy Spirit gives them special gifts, such as speaking in tongues. What do we think about that?

Is the principal work of the Holy Spirit to make Jesus feel nearer to a person?

Is the principal work of the Holy Spirit to move us to work for peace and justice?

Questions

1. What are some of the ways in which your church cultivates members' spiritual gifts? How could it be more intentional about this?

2. Do you see the Holy Spirit at work in your congregation? How?

3. Do you see the Holy Spirit at work in your own life? How?

4. How would you describe the different stages of the Christian life that you have experienced?

CHAPTER 7

LIVING OUT THE
CHRISTIAN LIFE

Opening Prayer: Lord God, you have made us to glorify you and enjoy you forever. May the communion that you offer us with your Son also guide us into deeper fellowship with the people around us. We pray for their needs as well as for our own. Help us do all that we can to further one another's material and spiritual well-being. In Christ's name, Amen.[1]

Martha: I love the worship, preaching, and adult education opportunities in our congregation. But sometimes I worry that we aren't very good at living out the gospel, once we leave and go back home.

Jerry: Perhaps we could encourage formation of small groups. Those who like could meet once a week in each other's homes, pray, study the Bible, and discuss how to be disciples at work and in the world.

Lisa: I hope that issues of money will be part of any discipleship program that we organize. We have people in the congregation who can barely make ends meet and others who are very well-to-do.

1. Based on WC 7.001 and 7.074.

Max: We need to talk not only about our members' personal use of money but also about our congregation's financial resources and needs. What does our church budget say about our priorities?

The confessions tell us that we begin a new life when we are joined to Jesus Christ. As Paul declares, "If anyone is in Christ, there is a new creation: everything old has passed away; see, everything has become new!" (2 Cor. 5:17). Through Christ and his death and resurrection, we receive not only forgiveness of sins but also a new way of life, the fruit of the Spirit: "love, joy, peace, patience, kindness, generosity, faithfulness, gentleness, and self-control" (Gal. 5:22–23). Our basic life orientation shifts from being selfishly centered on ourselves to serving God and our neighbor.

Christians do not rest content with the promise of salvation in Christ; rather, God's goodness to them in Christ moves them to express their faith in word and deed. To be sure, this new life does not come easily to us. We will work at it over a lifetime. Nevertheless, the fact that we continue to fall short of being what we are in Christ does not leave us depressed or discouraged but rather emboldens us to ask God to forgive us, correct us, and renew our efforts. The Christian life is not focused on the mistakes of the past. It looks confidently into the future.

Drawing on Scripture, the confessions offer us wise guidance for how to live out our new identity in Christ. They cannot tell us exactly what to do in a specific situation, but they do give us general trajectories for learning to live more faithfully as Christ's disciples, as when we make practical decisions about money.

The Reformation confessions follow Luther and Calvin in emphasizing that our salvation rests on Christ alone. He is our justification and sanctification. Nevertheless, the confessions also insist that faith sends us into action. The Second Helvetic Confession declares that we are given not "a fictitious, empty, lazy, and dead faith, but [rather] a living, quickening faith" (SH 5.111; the word "quickening" means enlivening); "man was not created or regenerated through faith in order to be idle, but rather that without ceasing he should do those things which are good and use-ful" (SH 5.118). The Scots Confession adds that "the Spirit of the Lord Jesus, who dwells in our hearts by true faith, brings forth such works as God has prepared for us to walk in" (SC 3.13).

Presbyterian theologian Brian Gerrish has proposed that "grace and gratitude" lie at the heart of Reformed piety.[2] He sees God's magnificent goodness as calling us into lives of hum-ble thanksgiving. The Heidelberg Catechism puts it this way: "[Christ is] restoring us by his Spirit into his image, so that with our whole life we may show that we are thankful to God . . . [and] so that he may be praised through us" (HC 4.086). The Second Helvetic Confession, too, speaks of good works as a means by which we show forth "gratitude to God" (SH 5.117; see also WC 6.088). Similarly, A Brief Statement of Faith tells us that "in gratitude to God, . . . we strive to serve Christ in our daily tasks" (BSF ##72–73).

Good works also help our neighbor (SH 5.117; see also HC 4.086 and WC 6.088). In the words of the Theological Declaration of Barmen, Christ offers us "a joyful deliverance from the fetters of this world for a free, grateful service to his creatures" (DB 8.14). A Brief Statement of Faith affirms this point while reflecting the contemporary psychological insight that only one who loves one-self is able to love others; hence, the Spirit "sets us free to accept ourselves and to love God and neighbor" (BSF #55).

Beyond showing gratitude to God and assisting other people, good works have yet a third aspect: to help us deepen our faith. This theme becomes more pronounced in the later Reformation documents, such as the Heidelberg Catechism, which tells us that we do good works "so that we may be assured of our faith by its fruits" (HC 4.086). The Westminster Confession of Faith, as we saw in chapter 5, gives even greater attention to the question of assurance through works, devoting an entire chapter to it (WC 6.097–109): All those who "truly believe in the Lord Jesus, and love him in sincerity, endeavoring to walk in all good conscience

2. See Brian Gerrish, *Grace and Gratitude: The Eucharistic Theology of John Calvin* (Minneapolis: Fortress, 1993).

before him, may in this life be certainly assured that they are in a state of grace" (WC 6.097).

Some theologians have accused the Westminster Confession of promoting morbid introspection. Rather than living with joy and confidence in Christ and his saving work, people become obsessed with their inner spiritual state and whether they are advancing or retreating in faith. Nevertheless, even for Westminster our ultimate goal is not to look at ourselves but rather to serve God and God's saving purposes. In the famous words of the first question of the Westminster Shorter Catechism, "Man's chief end is to glorify God, and to enjoy him forever" (WSC 7.001).

Our justification, God's forgiveness of us in Christ, does not free us from temptation and sin. Sanctification is a process of growing in holiness that will not reach completion in this life. And the same is true of our "good works." They are weak and flawed, and while we can make progress, we always fall short of God's law and Christ's example. Here the confessions are not denying that sinful people can do certain kinds of good (see SH 5.046 and WC 6.093). A musician can play an instrument with excellence. A businessperson can skillfully organize a project or a team. But according to the confessions we are incapable of fully repairing the breaches in relationship with God and others that have occurred and continue to occur because of our sinful self-centeredness.

The Scots Confession speaks of "the continual battle which is between the flesh and the Spirit in God's children" (SC 3.13). Further, "our nature is so corrupt, weak, and imperfect, that we are never able perfectly to fulfill the works of the law. Even after we are reborn, if we say that we have no sin, we deceive ourselves and the truth of God is not within us" (SC 3.15). Similarly, the Heidelberg Catechism declares that "even our best works in this life are imperfect and stained with sin" (HC 4.062). The Westminster Confession of Faith adds that even the most obedient Christians "fall short of much which in duty they are bound to do" (WC 6.090). The Confession of 1967 affirms that "the new life does not release a man from conflict with unbelief, pride, lust, fear. He still has to struggle with disheartening difficulties and problems" (C67 9.24).

No, our works cannot save us. The Westminster Confession reminds us that "when we have done all we can, we have done but our duty, and are unprofitable servants: . . . and as [our best works] . . . are defiled and mixed with so much weakness and imperfection, . . . they cannot endure the severity of God's judgment" (WC 6.091; see also SH 5.123). Whatever good resides in our works is due wholly to the Holy Spirit (WC 6.091).

God nevertheless accepts our works. The Scots Confession assures us that "as God the Father beholds us in the body of his Son Christ Jesus, he accepts our imperfect obedience as if it were perfect, and covers our works, which are defiled with many sins, with the righteousness of his Son" (SC 3.15). According to the Second Helvetic Confession, "God receives into favor and embraces those who do works for Christ's sake" (SH 5.122; see also SH 5.120 and WC 6.092). The Confession of 1967 similarly affirms that as a person matures "in his life with Christ, he lives in freedom and good cheer, . . . confident that the new life is pleasing to God and helpful to others" (C67 9.23). John Calvin once wrote that God takes delight in our efforts to live the Christian life, just as earthly parents smile with approval at a child who clumsily seeks to imitate them. The confessions, too, can say that God "rewards" us for our works, however imperfect they are (see SH 5.122 and WC 6.092).

God's justification and sanctification of our works allow us to live with the freedom of the children of God (see WC 6.108). Because we belong to God, we are not bound to any other power that would tell us the purpose of our lives or place us in its service. In the words of the Westminster Confession of Faith, "God alone is Lord of the conscience" (WC 6.109). But the confessions make clear that Christian freedom is not the freedom to do whatever we want. That would only be enslavement to our impulses and desires. Rather, our freedom is freedom "in the Lord," and we look to God to guide us in living out our new life in Jesus Christ.

The confessions identify two major guides to Christian discipleship and good works: God's law as first given in the Old Testament, and the life and teachings of Christ, which fulfill the law (see Matt. 5:17–18). The place of Old Testament law for Christians was a subject of controversy in the first years of the Christian church, and the apostle Paul argues against requiring Gentile Christians to be subject to Jewish circumcision or dietary regulations (see his Letter to the Galatians). The confessions are therefore careful to distinguish which Old Testament laws apply to Christians and which do not.

In line with typical Reformation discussions, the confessions speak of "ceremonial laws," which relate to Israel's worship; "judicial laws," which define Israel's form of government; and the "moral law," which directs Israel in its responsibilities to God and to humans (see WSC 6.101–3). The ceremonial and judicial laws were specific to Israel; only the moral law still applies to Christians. This moral law is summarized in the Decalogue (Ten Commandments), which is further summarized by Jesus' great commandment to "love the Lord your God with all your heart, . . . soul, . . . and mind, . . . and your neighbor as yourself" (Matt. 22:37–39). The first table of the Decalogue (the first four commandments) teaches us how to love God; the second table (the last six) relates us to our neighbor (see HC 4.093 and WLC 7.212).

Reformation theologians go on to identify three "uses" of the moral law: the accusatory use, by which people become aware of their sin and seek Christ's salvation (see WLC 7.205); the civil use, by which governments provide for what is just and right; and (in John Calvin's words) a "third use" specifically for believers. In its "third use," the moral law motivates and directs the good works that flow from the new selves that the Spirit is creating within us (see WLC 7.207). The Ten Commandments stimulate our good works in thankfulness to God for his saving work in Christ.

For the Second Helvetic Confession, the Old Testament moral law offers us "the patterns of virtues and vices" (SH 5.085) and "the pattern of good works" (SH 5.115). The Westminster Confession says that the law is "of great use" to believers because it is "a rule of life" that directs them in "the will of God and their duty" (WC 6.106). The Heidelberg Catechism places its discussion of the Ten Commandments under the heading of "Gratitude," because, according to the catechism, we express our thanks to God for our salvation by doing good works in accord with his commandments (HC 4.086). Other major discussions of the Decalogue appear in the Westminster Larger and Shorter Catechisms, where they explicate our duties of love to God and to each other (see the heading above WLC 7.201).

At first glance, the Ten Commandments seem too narrow in scope to guide the Christian life in all of its complexity. After all, few of us will be guilty—at least, not on a regular basis!—of murder, adultery, stealing, or false witness. But Reformation-era theologians, including Luther and Calvin, saw how Jesus' Sermon on the Mount made the commandments more broadly applicable:

[Jesus said,] "You have heard that it was said to the men of old, 'You shall not kill, and whoever kills shall be liable to judgment.' But I say to you that every one who is angry with his brother shall be liable to judgment; whoever insults his brother shall be liable to the council, and whoever says, 'You fool!' shall be liable to the hell of fire. So if you are offering your gift at the altar, and there remember that your brother has something against you, leave your gift there before the altar and go; first be reconciled to your brother, and then come and offer your gift." (Matt. 5:21–24 RSV)

Here Jesus makes three important moves. First, he broadens the commandment: "Do not kill" now means not even to insult your brother; after all, we can "kill" not only a person's body but also their spirit or reputation. Second, Jesus internalizes the commandment: We can fulfill "Do not kill" only if we do not harbor inner attitudes of anger or hatred toward others. Third, Jesus turns the negative prohibition into a positive injunction: "Do not kill" requires us actively to seek reconciliation with those who are estranged from us.

The catechisms in the *Book of Confessions* also make these three interpretive moves. The Heidelberg Catechism's interpretation of the sixth commandment provides an especially clear example. First, the commandment is broadened (see also WC 7.209 #6):

Q. 105: What is God's will for you in the sixth commandment?

A. I am not to belittle, hate, or insult, or kill my neighbor—not by my thoughts, my words, my look or gesture, and certainly not by actual deeds. . . . (HC 4.105)

Next, the commandment is internalized (see also WC 7.209 #2):

Q. 106: Does this commandment refer only to murder?

A. By forbidding murder God teaches us that he hates the root of murder: envy, hatred, anger, vindictiveness. . . . (HC 4.106)

Finally, the negative ("Thou shalt not") is turned into a positive ("Thou shalt") (see also WC 7.209 #4):

Q. 107: Is it enough then that we do not murder our neighbor in any such way?

A. No. By condemning envy, hatred, and anger God wants us to love our neighbors as ourselves, to be patient, peace-loving, gentle, merciful, and friendly toward them. . . . (HC 4.107)

Through this process of broadening, internalizing, and turning the negative into a positive (and vice versa), the commandments reach into every area of our lives. The Ten Commandments no longer define narrow, discrete actions (such as "Do not kill") but rather become comprehensive guides, both personally and socially, for living out our identity in Christ. In the words of the Second Helvetic Confession, "The whole will of God and all necessary precepts for every sphere of life are taught in this law" (SH 5.082). The Westminster Larger Catechism exemplifies the wide range of the commandments by providing long lists of desirable or undesirable behaviors under each. It is also noteworthy that the Larger Catechism identifies the positive duties of each commandment of the second table before listing the corresponding prohibitions.

Rather than explicating the Decalogue, the twentieth-century confessions look especially to the life and teachings of Jesus. The Declaration of Barmen calls Jesus Christ "God's mighty claim upon our whole life . . . for a free, grateful service to his creatures" (DB 8.14). The Confession of 1967 tells us that "the new life finds its direction in the life of Jesus, his deeds and words, his struggles against temptation, his compassion, his anger, and his willingness to suffer death. The teaching of apostles and prophets guides men in living this life" (C67 9.24). Similarly, "the life, death, resurrection, and promised coming of Jesus Christ has set the pattern for the church's mission" (C67 9.32). The Confession of 1967 adds that members of the community of faith assist each other in living out these ways of discipleship (C67 9.24).

The Confession of Belhar takes a slightly different tack. It delineates major ethical trajectories that run through the Old Testament and find their fulfillment in Christ: God "is in a special way the God of the destitute, the poor and the wrong" (Luke 6:20–26); "God brings justice to the oppressed . . . and bread to the hungry" (Luke 4:16–19); "God frees the prisoner and restores sight to the blind" (Luke 7:22); "God supports the downtrodden, protects the stranger, helps orphans and widows and blocks the path of the ungodly" (Ps. 146) (CB 10.7). And "God calls the church to follow God in this: . . . the church must stand where the Lord stands, namely against injustice and with the wronged" (Ps. 82:1–5) (CB 10.7).

The Ten Commandments, the example and teachings of Jesus, and broad biblical themes of justice and peace continue to be key resources for Christian discipleship today. They suggest key spiritual practices and disciplines that can help us grow more fully into the image of Christ. We cultivate a new set of attitudes and dispositions, the fruit of the Spirit to which Paul refers.

These practices and disciplines can shape us not only as individuals but also as communities of faith. Let us take the example of money. If, as Jesus says, "Where your treasure is, there your heart will be also" (Matt. 6:21), can the confessions help guide a church's budgeting process? Yes, indeed! Look at the eighth commandment. When broadened (the first step), "Do not steal," calls for avoiding personal excess and for fighting social injustice. The Heidelberg Catechism rejects, among other things, "fraudulent merchandising . . . [and] excessive interest" (HC 4.110). The Westminster Larger Catechism further condemns "receiving anything that is stolen, fraudulent dealing, . . . vexatious lawsuits, . . . engrossing commodities to enhance the price, . . . idleness, [and] prodigality" (WLC 7.252). More relevant to a congregation today may be Heidelberg's warning that "God forbids all greed and pointless squandering of his gifts" (HC 4.110; see also WLC 7.252).

When internalized (the second step), the commandment forbids "covetousness, . . . distrustful and distracting cares, . . . [and] envying . . . the prosperity of others" (WLC 7.252). And when the negative prohibition is expressed as a positive injunction (the third step), the commandment's concern for others' well-being becomes especially clear. According to the Heidelberg Catechism, God requires "that I do good whenever I can for my neighbor's good" (HC 4.111). Similarly, the Westminster Larger Catechism calls for "giving and lending freely, according to our abilities, . . . moderation of our judgments, wills, and affections, concerning worldly goods, . . . and an endeavor by all just and lawful means to procure, preserve, and further the wealth and outward estate of others, as well as our own" (WLC 7.251).

The twentieth-century confessions provide additional guidance. The Confession of 1967 identifies economics as an area in which the church is called to show forth Christ's reconciling ministry: "Because Jesus identified himself with the needy and exploited, the cause of the world's poor is the cause of his discipleship. . . . [The church] encourages those forces in human society that raise men's hopes for better conditions. . . . [A church] that is open to one social class only, or expects gratitude for its beneficence[,] makes a mockery of reconciliation" (C67 9.46). As we have seen, the Confession of Belhar also calls the church to stand by the poor and the needy. Moreover, says Belhar, "in following Christ the church must witness against all the powerful and privileged who seek their own interests and thus control and harm others" (CB 10.7).

Together, the confessions give us a large agenda, indeed more than we individually or corporately could ever accomplish. Yet the point of the confessional witness is not to make us feel helpless, but rather to stimulate our good works as expressions of thankfulness to God and of helpfulness to others. A congregation that is shaped by the confessions will be realistic about its financial needs yet not driven by them. It will not allow concerns about money to divert it from the ministry that God has given it. Every church has gifts, including financial resources, to further God's ways in the world.

When it comes to the needs of our congregations, we will be modest in our expenditures. But when it is a matter of serving others, especially the poor and the needy, we will be as generous as possible. Moreover, we will seek not simply to give money away, but also to use our resources to promote reconciliation. We will always be asking, How can we use our money to bring people together who otherwise have little to do with each other or may even look at each other suspiciously—the well-to-do and the not so well-to-do, members of different races and classes, or people who have become alienated from each other because of past hurts or present disagreements? Reconciliation within a congregation is as important as in society, for the church's witness depends on the character of the church's own life.

The apostle Paul sometimes compares the Christian life to a race (1 Cor. 9:24–27 and 2 Tim. 4:6–8; see also Heb. 12:1), and just like athletes, we must train long and hard in order to reach the finish line. But we do so out of a sense of thankfulness for our new life in Jesus Christ. The Spirit has given us a deep desire to draw closer to God and to each other.

The confessions point us to the patterns of faithful living that are defined by God's law for Israel, as it comes to its fulfillment in Christ. Our faith in him touches every area of our existence. Every part of us needs reformation; every part of us can be conformed more closely to his will. Personal and communal disciplines of prayer, worship, Scripture reading, and service help us along the way, as do the love and encouragement that we offer each other in the community of faith.

In the end, we will not look at ourselves and take pride in our achievements. Rather, we will give thanks that God has been able to use us for good, despite our sinfulness and our limitations. The God who reconciles us to himself through Jesus Christ impels us to seek reconciliation with others. We are privileged to share in his ministry—also in the way in which we use our money.

FOR DISCUSSION

Concerns Raised in the Opening Dialogue

We aren't very good at living out the gospel when we leave church and go home.

Could participation in a prayer or study group help a person grow in discipleship?

How can a congregation talk about the way in which disciples of Jesus Christ should use money?

How does a church budget reflect our priorities?

Questions

1. Discuss the meaning of the ninth commandment ("You shall not bear false witness"), using the three interpretive moves of the catechisms: broadening, internalizing, and turning the negative into a positive. Compare your answers with the Heidelberg Catechism 4.112 and the Westminster Larger Catechism 7.253–55.
2. What priorities are reflected in your church's budget? What does this say about your church?
3. How could your church use its financial resources to promote greater reconciliation within the congregation or in society?
4. What are some key disciplines of faith that your congregation could encourage its members to practice? How could you help people practice them?

CHAPTER 8

THE MEANING OF
CHURCH MEMBERSHIP

Opening Prayer: *O God, protect and preserve your church. Save it from all powers that would harm it, and allow us, its members, to grow in life together. Take away from us all blindness, weakness, reluctance, and hard-heartedness, and by your grace make us able and willing to know your will and to submit to it. Through your Son, Jesus Christ. Amen.*[1]

Martha: We often get visitors to our church, but we seem to have a hard time attracting them into membership.

Jerry: The new generation isn't interested in "joining" anything. So I say, if someone wants to come to church, great, let's welcome them. But the most important thing to me is whether people have love in their hearts.

Lisa: Well, I just don't know how people manage without a community of faith. I find so much emotional support here.

Max: It's easy to become a member of a church, but the apostle Paul says that to be a Christian is to be a

---

1. Based on WLC 7.173 and 7.302.

member of the body of Christ. What does that mean, and how can we explain it to the people in our next new members' class?

Since the early twenty-first century, sociologists of religion have identified a growing number of Americans as "nones," people who, when asked about their religious affiliation, state that they have "none." Few of the nones are atheists or agnostics. Many are interested in religious and spiritual insights. They believe in a God or some kind of higher spiritual power. But for them, belief and religious practice are private, personal matters. The nones do not see a reason to belong to a religious community or to adhere to the teachings and practices of a particular religious tradition. Some observers describe the nones as "spiritual but not religious." The nones "believe without belonging."

Many other people still search out a religious community in which to practice their faith. But even here religious loyalties are less stable than once upon a time. Contemporary Americans feel free to move from one church to another, based on what meets their needs at a particular time of life. They may have grown up Methodist but now live in a community where the Presbyterian Church has the best programs for their children. Or perhaps a man grew up Lutheran but married a Catholic woman, so now they attend Catholic mass together. And people move with increasing ease not only across denominational church lines but also between religions. A young person may choose to be Buddhist, after having been raised as a Christian. Or a marriage between a Christian and a Jew may result in their children attending some activities in a Christian church, while participating in other events in a Jewish temple.

American religion has often been characterized by an entrepreneurial spirit. New churches start up and attract people from other congregations. The demographic composition of a community may change, and older, established churches decline, while new churches—sometimes with new forms of worship and architecture—prosper. In recent years, nondenominational churches, megachurches, and house churches have become viable options next to traditional religious communities. The diversity of American religion responds to Americans' desire to make personal choices about faith. They do not go to church just because their parents did or because their neighbors do.

Freedom of choice is good not only for individuals but also for the church. When people come to church because they want to and not because they have to, they are more apt to be active participants, seeking to grow in faith. But freedom of choice also has a downside. Some people regularly attend a church but resist making a commitment to membership. Others become members only to quietly disappear after a few months. In such a time, congregations struggle to know how to design new members' classes. How many sessions should there be, and what should be covered? What kind of commitment can a congregation realistically expect of someone thinking about membership, and what kind of commitment is the congregation making to them? In a world of freedom of choice, we easily forget that Christian faith speaks a great deal about putting our own needs aside in order to serve God and other people. The church's one foundation is Christ, not personal or group interests.

The confessions help us understand the meaning of church membership by clarifying the nature and purpose of the church. The confessions offer us a basic vocabulary for describing the church's life, ministry, and mission, and the responsibilities of church members. While shifts in emphasis are evident over the centuries, the confessions consistently see the church as an institution that is defined not primarily by human needs and interests, but rather by God's work of salvation.

What kind of organization are people joining in the church? What makes the church "the church"? The Nicene Creed identifies four basic attributes (sometimes called "notes" or "marks") of the church: "one, holy, catholic, and apostolic." The Apostles' Creed repeats two of these attributes: the "holy catholic Church." Later confessions explicate one or more of the ancient notes.

The church is *one*. The Scots Confession declares that "from the beginning, there has been, now is, and to the end of the world

shall be, one Kirk, . . . one company and multitude of men chosen by God" (SC 3.16). Similarly, the Heidelberg Catechism says
that "from the beginning of the world to its end, [God] gathers,
protects, and preserves for himself a community chosen for eternal life and united in true faith" (HC 4.054; see also SH 5.124).
The church was not first born at Pentecost. Rather, it has existed
since Adam. It includes the people of Israel, who received the
promise of the coming Messiah. The Second Helvetic Confession
adds that although there are two Testaments, "All these people . . .
[are] one body under one Head, all united together in the same
faith" (SH 5.129).

For the Second Helvetic Confession, the church is one because
there is "one God"; "one mediator" Jesus Christ between God
and humanity, and "one Head" of the body; [and] "one Spirit,
one salvation, [and] one faith" (SH 5.126). Even when dissensions have arisen within the church, God has preserved its unity:
"There have at all times been great contentions in the Church,
and the most excellent teachers of the Church have differed
among themselves about important matters without meanwhile
the Church ceasing to be the Church because of these contentions" (SH 5.133). This perspective on unity can be reassuring to
us today. Despite the pain that congregational or denominational
controversy can leave in its wake, the Second Helvetic Confession is certain that "it pleases God to use the dissensions that arise
in the Church to the glory of his name, to illustrate the truth, and
in order that those who are in the right might be made manifest"
(1 Cor. 11:19)" (SH 5.133).

Unity does not preclude diversity. Many matters in church life
are "indifferent" and allow for a variety of opinions and practices.
The unity of the church is not based on "outward rites and cer-
emonies" (SH 5.141 and 5.241). But where "the true and harmonious preaching of the Gospel of Christ" (SH 5.141) is at stake,
the church must take a stand against heresy, as when the Second
Helvetic Confession condemns papal indulgences (SH 5.104; see
also SH 5.008; 5.019; and 5.035).

The Confession of 1967 reaffirms that unity includes certain
kinds of diversity: "The institutions of the people of God change

and vary as their mission requires in different times and places. The unity of the church is compatible with a wide variety of forms" (C67 9.34). But in contrast to the Reformation-era confessions, the Confession of 1967 does not emphasize resisting heresy, but rather speaks of practicing reconciliation, so that these institutional differences are not "allowed to harden into sectarian divisions, exclusive denominations, and rival factions" (C67 9.34).

Like the Confession of 1967, the Confession of Belhar bases church unity on Christ's reconciling work: "Christ's work of reconciliation is made manifest in the church as the community of believers who have been reconciled with God and with one another. . . . Unity is, therefore, both a gift and an obligation for the church. . . . Through the working of God's Spirit [unity] is a binding force, yet simultaneously a reality which must be earnestly pursued and sought" (CB 10.3).

This kind of reconciliation is much more than just agreeing to disagree when essential matters of faith are at stake. The call to reconciliation in the Confessions of 1967 and Belhar rests on biblical and historic truths that the older confessions seek to secure: God's creation of humanity for communion with God; humanity's sinful rebellion against God; the life and work of Christ, who as the God-man restores the possibility of communion between God and humanity; and the Spirit's work of applying Christ's benefits to believers within a community of faith. Commitment to these truths will require the church to take a stand against dissenting positions, even while expressing love to those who represent them. The church nevertheless trusts that unity is finally not its achievement but rather God's. God has protected and cared for his church "since the beginning of the world and will do [so] to the end" (CB 10.1).

In explicating the other three notes of the church, the confessions offer less detail. Just as the unity of the church is established ultimately in and through Christ, the church is *holy* because of Christ's holiness and his sanctifying work (SH 5.125). The church is *catholic*, "that is, universal, because it contains the chosen of all ages, of all realms, nations, and tongues" (SC 3.16). It "is scattered through all parts of the world . . . and is not limited to any times or places" (SH 5.126).

The fourth note, "apostolic," is hardly mentioned at all. The Reformation-era documents reject the Roman Catholic understandings of apostolicity, according to which the faith of the church has been handed down by an unbroken line of bishops going back to the first disciples. The Scots Confession argues that the true church is not established by "antiquity, usurped title, [or] lineal succession" (SC 3.18; see also SH 5.135). By implication, what makes the church apostolic is its proclamation of the gospel. The Confession of 1967 directly states this Protestant understanding of apostolicity: "The church maintains continuity with the apostles and with Israel by faithful obedience to [God's] call" to go into the world as God's reconciling community (C67 9.31).

In the Apostles' Creed, confession of the "holy catholic Church" is followed by belief in "the communion of saints" (AC 2.3). The idea of the church as a communion of saints reinforces the four notes of the Nicene Creed and especially the church's holiness and unity. As a communion of saints, believers are *holy ones*, "citizens of the heavenly Jerusalem" (SC 3.16), and these holy ones are *one in Christ*. They share "in all [of Christ's] treasures and gifts" (HC 4.055) and "have the fruit of inestimable benefits, one God, one Lord Jesus Christ, one faith" (SC 3.16). Believers are also *one with each other*. Each member is called to use their gifts "readily and joyfully for the service and enrichment of the other members" (HC 4.055). These gifts are not only spiritual, such as "mutual edification," but also material, such as relieving "each other in outward things" (WC 6.146–47). As in the early church, believers today should share all that they have with each other (see Acts 4:32), although the Westminster Confession of Faith is quick to add that the communion of saints does not abolish the right to private property (WC 6.148).

Among the twentieth-century confessions, it is especially the Confession of Belhar that picks up these themes of communion and sharing: As "one holy, universal Christian church, the communion of saints called from the entire human family, . . . we are obligated to give ourselves willingly and joyfully to be of benefit and blessing to one another" (CB 10.3). "We bear one another's burdens, . . . upbuild one another, . . . [and] suffer with one another" (CB 10.4).

Other biblical images further define the nature and purpose of the church. Paul's designation of the church as the "body of Christ" is especially important (see SC 3.16; SH 5.130; WC 6.140; and BSF #57). The Reformation-era confessions frequently include a second Pauline image: the church as the bride or spouse of Christ (SC 3.16; SH 5.130; and WC 6.140). Other images drawn from Scripture include a "temple of the living God" and a "flock of sheep" (SH 5.130), the "Kingdom of the Lord Jesus Christ" and the "house and family of God" (WC 6.141), and "the salt of the earth and the light of the world" (CB 10.5).

In addition, the confessions discuss where the one, holy, catholic, and apostolic church manifests itself. Two pairs of terms from the Reformation-era confessions provide guidance: visible/invisible and militant/triumphant. The invisible church is composed of "the whole number of the elect, that have been, are, or shall be gathered into one" (WC 6.140). They "truly know and rightly worship and serve the true God . . . [and] are partakers of all benefits which are freely offered through Christ" (SH 5.125; see also SC 3.16). In contrast, the visible church consists of all those (along with their children) who publicly profess the Christian religion (WC 6.141). Thus, the invisible church is pure, while the visible church has both "wheat" and "tares" (a reference to Matt. 13:24–30).

The confessions emphasize that as humans we do not have the ability on earth to distinguish these two groups (see SH 5.055 and 5.140). Only God knows who within the visible church truly believes in him and who does not. Even when the Christian community seems completely compromised by its members' sinfulness or crushed by its enemies, we can be certain that God nevertheless preserves a visible church on earth (SH 5.138).

"Militant" and "triumphant" refer to two dimensions of the invisible church (see SC 3.16 and SH 5.127). The church militant refers to the invisible church on earth, while the church triumphant is the church beyond time and space. While on earth, the elect are militant because they must continually do battle against powers of sin and evil. The church triumphant is composed of those elect who have passed from this life into heaven, where they have triumphed "immediately after having overcome all those things" and now "[rejoice] before the Lord" (SH 5.129).

Contemporary Americans are tempted to believe that what really matters is not participation in the visible church, but rather what is in your heart. If you believe in God, you will be "good with God" (in the church's traditional language, you will be among "the elect" in the "invisible church"). But on the whole the confessions take the opposite position, asserting that we need the visible church. In the words of the Second Helvetic Confession, "We esteem fellowship with the true Church of Christ so highly that we deny that those can live before God who do not stand in fellowship with the true Church of God, but separate themselves from it" (SH 5.136). The Westminster Confession of Faith declares that the visible church "is essential to [our] best growth and service" (WC 6.141). The Confession of 1967 states that in the church we gather "to enjoy fellowship, to receive instruction, strength, and comfort, . . . [and] to be tested, renewed, and reformed" (C67 9.36). It is in the visible church that we grow spiritually and become a communion of saints.

Perhaps for this reason, recent confessions abandon the distinction between invisible and visible. The church *is* the visible church. As the Declaration of Barmen insists, "The Christian Church is the congregation of the brethren in which Jesus Christ acts presently as the Lord in Word and Sacrament through the Holy Spirit" (DB 8.17). The Confession of 1967 has a similar emphasis: The church exists where "its members are both gathered in corporate life and dispersed in society for the sake of mission in the world" (C67 9.35). There is no invisible church concealed within or behind the visible church.

The question for the confessions is not how to find a church composed only of the morally pure. Every church on earth will be a mixture of faithful and faithless people, of true believers and insincere or false ones. Besides, each of us is both sinner and saint. But the confessions do ask us to shape our congregations to be as faithful as possible to God. How can we best be true to the oneness, holiness, catholicity, and apostolicity that God has bestowed on us?

This question became especially acute at the time of the Reformation. On the one hand, Luther and Calvin sought to justify why they had broken away from the Roman Catholic Church, and on the other, to help their followers recognize which of the many new Protestant churches were faithful to the gospel of Jesus Christ and which were distorting it. Luther identified seven "marks of the church": the Word of God, baptism, the Lord's Supper, confession and absolution (the "keys of the church"), ordained ministry, common worship, and suffering for the sake of Christ. Calvin set forth two marks: "Wherever we see the Word of God purely preached and heard, and the sacraments administered according to Christ's institution, there, it is not to be doubted, a church of God exists."[2]

The documents in the *Book of Confessions* build on these foundations. The Scots Confession affirms Calvin's two marks, while adding a third: "ecclesiastical discipline uprightly ministered, as God's Word prescribes, whereby vice is repressed and virtue nourished" (SC 3.18; see also HC 4.085). The Second Helvetic Confession, like Luther, refers to a wide set of activities that define the true church—common worship, repentance of sins, persevering in mutual love and peace, and participating in the sacraments (SH 5.135)—but especially emphasizes Calvin's first mark: "the lawful and sincere preaching of the Word of God as it was delivered to us in the books of the prophets and the apostles, which all lead us unto Christ" (SH 5.134). The Declaration of Barmen reaffirms Calvin's two marks when it states that the Lord is present to a congregation through "Word and Sacrament" (DB 8.17).

These lists do not represent an exhaustive list of activities necessary for the church to be "the church," but they do identify essential ministries that set forth Jesus Christ as Lord and Savior. The church is true to its calling to be one, holy, catholic, and apostolic when it proclaims God's free grace in Christ. The

2. John Calvin, *Institutes of the Christian Religion* 4.1.9, ed. John T. McNeill, trans. Ford Lewis Battles, Library of Christian Classics 20–21 (Philadelphia: Westminster Press, 1960).

church is faithful to Christ's saving work when its preaching and sacraments assure us that even though our lives individually and communally fall short of God's will, God continues to offer us forgiveness and renewal.

Other church activities should flow from, and back into, the ministry of Word and sacrament. This is especially true of church discipline. Too often in Reformed history—as classically portrayed in Nathaniel Hawthorne's *The Scarlet Letter*—religious authorities have wielded discipline in ways that violated people and alienated them from the church rather than assisted them to grow in faith. A view of discipline as church judicial proceedings and punishments is too narrow. Today many theologians helpfully speak, instead, of key spiritual "disciplines"—such as prayer, Sabbath-keeping, and almsgiving—that help believers practice the Christian life.[3] That kind of "discipline" draws us more fully into the ways of Christ, whom we encounter in Word and sacrament.

The confessions emphasize the special responsibility of ministers for the church's work. To be sure, all Christians are "priests" because God has freed us to pray directly to him; we do not need human intercessors, such as Mary and the saints (see SH 5.153). However, not all Christians are "ministers," but only those individuals who have been called and elected by the church (in the Presbyterian tradition, through acts of ordination and installation).

Drawing on Ephesians 4:11, the Second Helvetic Confessions gives these ministers various titles: "apostles, prophets, evangelists, bishops, elders, pastors, and teachers" (SH 5.147). They should be "distinguished by sufficient consecrated learning, pious eloquence, simple wisdom, lastly, by moderation and an honorable reputation" (SH 5.150). Further, they should "fear God, be constant in prayer, attend to spiritual reading, and in all things and at all times be watchful, and by a purity of life . . . shine before all [people]" (SH 5.164). As we have seen, A Brief Statement of Faith declares that God calls not only men but also "women . . . to all ministries of the Church" (BSF #64).

3. See Dorothy C. Bass, ed., *Practicing Our Faith* (San Francisco: Jossey-Bass, 1997).

The Second Helvetic Confession explains that while "the duties of ministers are various, . . . for the most part they are restricted to two, in which all the rest are comprehended: to the teaching of the Gospel of Christ, and to the proper administration of the Sacraments" (SH 5.163). The confession also emphasizes ministers' responsibility for church discipline, both in the narrower sense of imposing "discipline" (SH 5.165) and in the broader sense of cultivating "disciplines" of the Christian life, such as caring for the poor, visiting the sick, resisting temptation, praying, and fasting ("holy abstinence") (SH 5.163). By subjecting themselves to God's Word and to each other's counsel and discipline (SH 5.160 and 5.167), ministers show forth God's will, not their own (SH 5.156). Their authority is "more like a service than a dominion" (SH 5.159; see also DB 8.20).

More than the Reformation-era documents, the twentieth-century confessions make clear that ordained ministry serves the ministry of the whole people of God. As the Theological Declaration of Barmen states, "The various offices in the Church . . . are for the exercise of the ministry entrusted to and enjoined upon the whole congregation" (DB 8.20). Ministry is not restricted to ordained ministers; rather, it is the calling of every member of the church. The Confession of 1967 acknowledges that certain people are called and trained for "leadership and oversight" (C67 9.39) but insists that all members are responsible for ministry (C67 9.40): "Each member is the church in the world, endowed by the Spirit with some gift of ministry" (C67 9.38). The church serves "God wherever its members are, at work or play, in private or in the life of society. Their prayer and Bible study are part of the church's worship and theological reflection. Their witness is the church's evangelism" (C67 9.37).

Church membership is not primarily a matter of being listed on a membership roll or of making financial contributions. Rather, membership has to do with participation in the visible church and its ministries. On the one hand, we need the visible church because it is there that we are called again and again through Word and sacrament into life in Christ, and it is there that we practice being the communion of saints, the body of Christ. On the other hand, the visible church needs us. Each of us is a minister, because each of us has gifts for ministry. Not all of us will preach or administer the sacraments, but all of us are called to proclaim the gospel through our work and behavior in the world.

People may resist joining a church because they are not prepared to make these commitments. But people may also stay away if they do not clearly sense that the church is committed to them. Key questions for any congregation include the following: How can we better reach out to those who come to us—and to those who do not? Do we recognize and support each other in our gifts for ministry? Do we demonstrate that we are a community that seeks to be one, holy, catholic, and apostolic? Are Word and sacrament at the center of our life? Are we practicing a disciplined way of life?

God does not depend on the church to fulfill his purposes (see SH 5.137), but we do believe that he has given the church a special commission. In an era of the "nones," the church is most truly the church as it accepts the joys and burdens of shaping what Dietrich Bonhoeffer called "life together": a community shaped by Word and sacrament for the sake of love and service.

FOR DISCUSSION

Concerns Raised in the Opening Dialogue

It is difficult today to get people to join a church.

Is it enough for a person to love Jesus in their heart? Does everyone need the church?

Don't people need the emotional support that a community of faith provides?

What is church membership all about?

Questions

1. How would you explain to people in a new members' class what it means to join the church? How are members responsible to the church, and how is the church responsible to them?

2. How does your church encourage every member to be a "minister"? What else could the church be doing?
3. Why is church unity important? How could you promote unity not only within your congregation, but also with other Christian churches?
4. Which activities of the church are most important to you personally? How does your list compare with what the confessions say about the church's nature and purpose?

CHAPTER 9

PREPARING FOR BAPTISMS
AND SUPPORTING
THE BAPTIZED

Opening Prayer: Great God, we thank you for the gift of baptism, in which Jesus forgives us our sins yet lays your mighty claim upon our whole life. Call us back to the identity that you gave us at the font, that we would be free for grateful service to you and all your creatures. In the name of the Father, and the Son, and the Holy Spirit. Amen.[1]

Martha: Whenever we baptize babies, we vow to guide and nurture them as they grow up, to encourage them to follow Christ, and to be faithful members of his church. But I worry that we don't follow through very well.

Jerry: It's hard to keep track of the people in our congregation; we're all so busy. Maybe it would be better to baptize children after they've grown up a bit and can demonstrate that they are serious about their faith.

Lisa: Frankly, I've never quite gotten the point about baptism. It seems to me that what matters is whether

---

1. Based on DB 8.14.

people give their lives to Jesus, not whether they
have water sprinkled on their head.

Max: Well, I think baptism is a wonderful way to welcome
new children and adults into our fellowship.

In chapter 6, we noted that the Holy Spirit makes Christ's benefits "effectual" for us. Through the Holy Spirit, we are united to
the living, resurrected Christ and share in his life. We undergo
a process of transformation (sanctification). In this chapter, we
explore the "outward means" by which the Spirit does this work.
Just as God uses the visible church to call us into Christ's way of
life, so too God uses visible signs, such as baptism and the Lord's
Supper, to touch us with his grace and change us. John Calvin
observed that humans are composed not only of a mind or spirit
but also of a body. As physical beings, we are responsive to material things. The sacraments have a special power for us because
they use material elements—water, bread, and wine—to communicate God's grace to us. These physical signs reinforce, seal, and
confirm God's promises to us in the gospel.

The sacrament of baptism is of special interest—and confusion—
in the church today. Some Christian traditions, such as Baptist, do
not regard baptism as a sacrament, but rather as an "ordinance."
It is something that we do because it has been ordained or ordered
by God, but it does not communicate God's grace in any special
way. In addition, Baptist churches baptize only people who have
first made a public declaration of their faith in Jesus Christ, which
rules out infants and small children. This theology of baptism has
influenced much of North American Protestantism. Even people
who attend churches in the Reformed tradition may ask that we
"dedicate" rather than baptize their children, leaving the children
to decide later and for themselves whether or not to be baptized.
The American spirit of individualism and personal choice may
reinforce this attitude.

Other Christian traditions, such as Catholic, have a very different understanding. For them, a person's salvation depends on
baptism. A child should be baptized as soon as possible after birth;
if it appears that the infant is close to death and a priest is not

nearby, a nurse, a midwife, or another layperson may perform the baptism. According to Catholic theology, baptism washes away the original sin that clings to the soul of every human, including newborn babies. Baptism immediately justifies and sanctifies us. This approach, while so different from Baptist theology, has been no less influential on many Americans. People sometimes come to our churches asking us to baptize their babies as a spiritual safety measure. These people may not be sure that baptism really does anything, but they don't want to take any chances.

Other motives may be at work when someone requests baptism. A couple may desire that their child be baptized not because they care about baptism but rather because they wish to please grandma or grandpa. Alternatively, an adult may have been baptized as a child but asks to be baptized again because only now have they made a conscious commitment to Christ. Or one may have once been baptized but then fell away from the church and now wishes to recommit oneself to Christ.

A baptism is almost always a special moment in the life of a congregation. People take delight in watching parents bring their baby forward to be baptized and welcomed into the community of faith. We admire adults who stand before us to be baptized because they have made a commitment to Christ. But just what is God doing in a baptism? Is baptism essential for a person's salvation, or is it just a ritual that helps people celebrate their commitments to each other? Should a pastor or session ever refuse a request for baptism? We turn again to the confessions for guidance.

The confessions speak of two principal means through which the Holy Spirit works to bring people into life in Christ: the preached word and the sacraments. As the Heidelberg Catechism declares, "The Holy Spirit produces [faith] in our hearts by the preaching of the holy gospel, and confirms it by the use of the holy sacraments" (HC 4.065; see also WC 7.088, which adds "prayer"). The Second Helvetic Confession acknowledges "that God can illuminate whom and when he will, even without the external ministry" (SH 5.007). But it and the other confessions affirm that God normally uses the church and its ministry of Word and sacrament to bring people to faith.

Preaching and the sacraments are closely related. While the confessions acknowledge the value of reading Scripture on our own, they insist that we also need the church's preaching and sacraments to help us rightly interpret the Bible. God uses the preached Word and the sacraments to "accommodate" himself to our human weakness, so that he does not overwhelm us with his power and glory but rather draws near in love and mercy.

According to the Westminster Larger Catechism, preaching aims at "enlightening, convincing, and humbling sinners, of driving them out of themselves, and drawing them unto Christ, [and] of conforming them to his image" (WLC 7.265). The Confession of 1967 makes a similar point: "Through preaching . . . the people hear the Word of God and accept and follow Christ" (C67 9.49). This kind of preaching makes demands on both the preacher and the people. For their part, preachers will take into consideration "the necessities and capacities of the hearers" (WLC 7.269). "The message is addressed to men in particular situations . . . [and] should be conducive to men's hearing of the gospel in a particular time and place" (C67 9.49). For their part, the hearers will "attend upon [the preaching] with diligence, preparation, and prayer . . . and readiness of mind, as the Word of God" (WLC 7.270).

The sacraments have the same function: to touch us with Christ's grace in the particular circumstances of our lives. The sacraments "seal and confirm [the Word and promise of God] in our hearts" (SC 3.18; see also HC 4.066; SH 5.169; and WC 6.149). Moreover, like preaching, the sacraments become effectual for us only by the power of the Holy Spirit, as it awakens in us faith in God's promises (see SC 3.21 and SH 5.183).

The confessions declare that Christ instituted two sacraments: baptism and the Lord's Supper (SC 3.21; SH 5.178; and WLC 2.274). The Second Helvetic Confession defines sacraments as "mystical symbols, or holy rites, or sacred actions, instituted by God himself, consisting of his Word, of signs and of things signified" (SH 5.159; see also WLC 2.273). Words and signs work together to set forth a sacrament's meaning. At the time of a baptism or the Lord's Supper, the minister speaks words—words that the people hear and understand—that declare what God has done and is still doing, while the physical signs and outward actions of the sacraments make the meaning of these words clearer and more relevant to us. Here the Reformation-era confessions are reacting against a medieval Catholicism in which people did not understand the Latin words of the Mass, and the sacramental signs seemed to function as magical actions (see SC 3.22).

The sacraments, first of all, set forth God and God's promises to us. As we noticed above, the sacraments confirm and seal the promises of God that the preached Word sets forth. The Scots Confession tells us that God uses the sacraments "to exercise the faith of his children and . . . to seal in their hearts the assurance of his promise, and of that most blessed conjunction, union, and surety, which the chosen have with their Head" (SC 3.21). For the Heidelberg Catechism, the sacraments confirm "that our entire salvation rests on Christ's one sacrifice for us on the cross" (HC 4.067). The Second Helvetic Confession declares that the principal "thing which God promises in all Sacraments and to which all the godly direct their attention . . . is Christ the Savior—the only sacrifice" (SH 5.175). According to the Westminster Confession of Faith, the sacraments "represent Christ and his benefits, and . . . confirm our interest in him" (WC 6.149).

But the sacraments have a second trajectory, as well: to point us to each other and our responsibilities to the world. As regards the church, the Scots Confession notes that the sacraments "make a visible distinction between [God's] people and those who were without the Covenant" (SC 3.21; see also SH 5.169 and WC 6.149). Further, the Westminster Larger Catechism tells us that as a covenant community, we are obliged "to testify and cherish [our] love and communion one with another" (WLC 7.272). The Westminster Confession of Faith adds that the sacraments "engage [us] to the service of God" (WC 6.149). As regards the world, the Confession of 1967 emphasizes that the sacraments strengthen the church's "service of God among men" (C67 9.49). By drawing us into the life of Christ, baptism and the Lord's Supper move us to seek reconciliation both within the church and in the world.

These insights from the confessions about the sacraments in general help us better understand the sacrament of baptism in particular. Words of promise based on Scripture are joined to the outward sign of water, and the outward sign sets forth and clarifies the promises, so that they touch us more deeply than words alone do. Moreover, the promises attached to baptism point us in two directions: toward God and his claim on us, and toward each other and the world around us. While faith, not baptism, is necessary for salvation, baptism is such a great help to us that we should not neglect it (see WC 6.158).

As for God's promises, baptism especially represents forgiveness. The Scots Confession tells us that through baptism our sins "are remitted" (SC 3.21; see also WC 6.154). The Heidelberg Catechism speaks of "the washing away of sins" (HC 4.071). According to the Second Helvetic Confession, to be baptized is "to be cleansed also from the filthiness of sins" (SH 5.187). Water applied to a person's body helps dramatize this cleansing: "As surely as water washes away the dirt from the body, so certainly [Christ's] blood and his Spirit wash away my soul's impurity, that is, all my sins" (HC 4.069).

A second set of promises relates to rebirth or regeneration. The Heidelberg Catechism teaches that through baptism we are "renewed and sanctified . . . to be members of Christ, so that more and more we become dead to sin and live holy and blameless lives" (HC 4.070). The Second Helvetic Confession declares that in baptism "we are regenerated, purified, and renewed by God through the Holy Spirit" (SH 5.187). According to the Westminster Confession of Faith, baptism is a sign and seal of "regeneration . . . and of [one's] giving up unto God, through Jesus Christ, to walk in newness of life" (WC 6.154). The Confession of 1967 tells us that baptism represents "not only a cleansing from sin, but [also] a dying . . . [and] rising with Christ" (C67 9.51). Just as water refreshes the body physically, the waters of baptism revive us spiritually (see SH 5.188).

Still other promises refer to the new identity that baptism bestows on us. The Heidelberg Catechism assures us that by baptism "we are included in God's covenant and people" (HC 4.074;

see also WC 6.154). According to the Confession of 1967, "In baptism, the church celebrates the renewal of the covenant with which God has bound his people to himself" (C67 9.51). The Second Helvetic Confession tells us that in baptism we are "adopted" into the family of God (SH 5.186–87) and separated "from all strange religions and people" (SH 5.189). Several confessions also promise us that through baptism the Holy Spirit "engrafts" us into Christ (SC 3.21 and WC 6.154). As with cleansing and renewal, water helps make this promise of new life in Christ clearer. When we shower or bathe, water covers us; in a similar way, the waters of baptism cover us with Christ.

Next to the promises that relate us to God are promises—and responsibilities—that relate us to each other within and beyond the community of faith. The Second Helvetic Confession tells us that we are obligated by virtue of our baptism to "concur [with all members of the church] in the one religion and mutual services," while we fight against sin and evil in the world (SH 5.189). The Confession of 1967 declares that baptism "commits all Christians to die each day to sin and to live for righteousness. . . . By baptism, individuals are publicly received into the church to share in its life and ministry, and the church becomes responsible for their training and support in Christian discipleship" (C67 9.51). Baptism calls us into a different way of life with God, with each other, and in the world.

The confessions see baptism as a spiritual event in which God makes promises to us and we respond by committing ourselves to God and God's ways. But then there is the question of baptizing infants, who, so far as we can tell, cannot yet understand God's promises or respond to them. Do those parents who wish to delay baptism of their children have a valid point? Why has the Reformed tradition affirmed baptism of infants, even though they cannot yet profess their faith, obey God, or serve others?

At the time of the Reformation, groups known as Anabaptists (those who "baptize again") insisted on baptizing adult Christians who had already been baptized as infants but were only now making a public profession of faith. The Anabaptists viewed baptism primarily as a way of marking a person's conscious choice to follow Christ and to join the church and its alternative way of life.

Reformed confessions consistently reject this position (see SC 3.23 and SH 5.192), justifying the baptism of infants by appealing to the covenant that God has made with his people.

The Heidelberg Catechism declares that "infants as well as adults are included in God's covenant and people, and they, no less than adults, are promised deliverance from sin" (HC 4.074). The Second Helvetic Confession recalls Jesus' words that children belong to the kingdom of heaven (Matt. 19:14) (SH 5.192). The Westminster Larger Catechism affirms that "infants descending from parents, either both or but one of them, professing faith in Christ, and obedience to him, are, in that respect, within the covenant, and are to be baptized" (WLC 7.276; see also WC 6.157). And because infants belong to the covenant community, the members of the church have responsibilities to them. As the Confession of 1967 declares, "The congregation, as well as the parents, has a special obligation to nurture [infants] in the Christian life, leading them to make, by a public profession, a personal response to the love of God shown forth in their baptism" (C67 9.51).

What if a person falls away from their baptismal identity? Can a baptism ever fail "to take"? And if so, may a baptized person who returns to faith after falling away be baptized again? The confessions see baptism as a onetime event in which Christ's death and resurrection are represented as sufficient once and for all for human salvation. Christ's saving work is not deficient. It does not need to be repeated. At the same time, the confessions recognize that the "efficacy of Baptism is not tied to that moment of time wherein it is administered" (WC 6.159). A person who falls "short of, and [walks] contrary to, the grace of Baptism" that they have received (WLC 7.277) needs not a second baptism but rather a return to the promises of the first. In the words of the Westminster Larger Catechism, "The needful but much neglected duty of improving our Baptism, is to be performed by us all our life long, especially in the time of temptation" (WLC 7.277). The catechism adds that seeing the baptism of others can stir us up to reclaim our own baptismal identity (WLC 2.777).

As far as Reformed confessions are concerned, the sacraments are more than human rituals by which we attest our faith in Christ and are joined to a congregation (the Baptist position). Rather, God comes to us in a special way in the sacraments. But the confessions also reject the idea that the physical signs attached to the sacraments are somehow transformed into supernatural matter (the medieval Catholic position). For us, the waters of baptism remain water; the bread and wine of the Lord's Supper remain bread and wine. The confessions differ, however, in their explanations of just how God is present when we celebrate the sacraments.

For the Second Helvetic Confession, the Holy Spirit gives us grace inwardly at the very moment that we receive the sacraments outwardly. In regard to baptism, the confession declares that "inwardly we are regenerated, purified, and renewed by God through the Holy Spirit; and outwardly we receive the assurance of the greatest gifts in the water, by which also those great benefits are represented, and, as it were, set before our eyes to be beheld" (SH 5.187). Something similar occurs when the Word is preached or the Lord's Supper is celebrated: The inward work of the Holy Spirit occurs *parallel* to the outward actions of the church (see SH 5.005 and 5.196).

The Westminster Confession of Faith sometimes sounds like the Second Helvetic Confession. There is a parallel process: As we outwardly participate in the sacraments, God's grace touches us inwardly (WC 6.167). However, the Westminster Confession especially emphasizes that the sacraments *point us* to what God has done and is doing in Christ. They "represent Christ and his benefits" (WC 6.149). They are "a sign and seal of the covenant of grace, of [one's] ingrafting into Christ" (WC 6.154). "Grace . . . is exhibited in or by the sacraments" (WC 6.151). Moreover, when speaking of baptism, Westminster adds that this grace is not only exhibited but also *conferred* by the Holy Spirit (WC 6.159).

The Scots Confession comes closest to John Calvin's position that the sacraments are "means of grace" (though it does not use this term), that is, instruments by which God the Father through the Holy Spirit *unites* us to his Son, the crucified and risen Jesus Christ. The sacraments do not merely represent outwardly what the

Holy Spirit does inwardly, nor do they merely exhibit God's grace. Rather, God is really doing something to us spiritually *through* and *by means of* the physical signs attached to baptism and the Lord's Supper. The Scots Confession declares that "we utterly condemn the vanity of those who affirm the sacraments to be nothing else than naked and bare signs. No, we assuredly believe that by Baptism we are engrafted into Christ Jesus, to be partakers of his righteousness, by which our sins are covered and remitted" (SC 3.21).

In sum, the *Book of Confessions* is not of one mind about how God is present in or through the sacraments. While agreeing that the sacraments "represent" God's grace, the confessions leave open the question of just how. Nor do the twentieth-century confessions provide definitive resolution. Like the Westminster Confession of Faith, the Confession of 1967 speaks of "representation" without defining it further: "Baptism with water represents . . . cleansing, . . . dying . . . [and] rising" (C67 9.51). A Brief Statement of Faith simply states that the Spirit "claims us in the waters of baptism" (BSF #62). Recent Reformed liturgical resources, such as the Presbyterian *Directory for Worship* and the *Book of Common Worship*, have, however, been influenced by Calvin's conviction that the sacraments are means of grace that unite us to the living Christ.

In an era in which we often see baptism as a way of making a statement about ourselves—our profession of faith, our hopes for our children, or our desire as congregations to welcome and incorporate new members—the confessions challenge us to think about what God is doing in the sacraments. What is God promising us? How is Jesus Christ drawing us into his resurrection life? How is the Holy Spirit renewing us?

As we have seen, salvation does not depend on baptism, yet baptism is God's great gift to us, and we will want it for ourselves and our children. The sacrament of baptism can strengthen our faith, which is constantly under assault from doubt, temptation, and everyday trials and difficulties. When we remember that we have been baptized—as when we confess our sins or participate in the baptism of others—God's forgiving and renewing grace can again touch us and renew us.

Our baptismal liturgies will be strong when they focus less on the beauty of a new baby or the commitment of an adult convert to Christ, and more on God's saving work in Jesus Christ. Through baptism, we participate in his death and resurrection. Baptism therefore makes demands on us. It calls us to die to everything that separates us from Christ. It asks us to work over a lifetime to grow into the identity that Christ has already given us. Moreover, baptism of infants can have integrity only if parents and congregations follow through on their commitments to each other and to the children in their midst. That is hard work in a world in which people in churches easily come and go, and in which church leaders get so busy with administrative duties that they neglect their spiritual responsibilities.

Yes, a church that practices baptism must be ready for its demands. But baptism is not only demanding; it is also wonderful. It is wonderful because it sets forth to us God's free grace — the amazing truth that God accepts us and reconciles us to himself before we do anything to deserve it. Baptism teaches us more deeply than words alone that we and our children belong to God no matter what — no matter whether we or they grow in faith or fall short, no matter what hardships we or they endure, and no matter what other powers or principalities try to claim us or them. Baptism dramatically assures us, in the words of the Heidelberg Catechism, that "I am not my own, but belong — body and soul, in life and in death — to my faithful Savior Jesus Christ. . . . Because I belong to him, Christ, by his Holy Spirit, assures me of eternal life and makes me wholeheartedly willing and ready from now on to live for him" (HC 4.001).

FOR DISCUSSION

Concerns Raised in the Opening Dialogue

Do congregations follow through on their vows to guide and nurture those who are baptized?

Would it be better to wait until children can choose baptism for themselves?

Is baptism just an empty ritual?

Is baptism primarily about welcoming people into the community of faith?

Questions

1. The confessions speak of baptism as cleansing, death and resurrection, and new identity. Which of these meanings may be new to you? How do they help you think about baptism in a new way?

2. How can a congregation keep its promises to those whom it baptizes? What could a session or board of deacons do?

3. How should your church respond to a request for a "rebaptism"?

4. How can we celebrate a baptism in a way that opens us more fully to what God is doing and promising?

CHAPTER 10

CELEBRATING THE LORD'S SUPPER AND LIVING IN COMMUNITY

Opening Prayer: God our Creator and Redeemer, we pray that our hearts may be lifted up to Jesus Christ. Apply to us the benefits of his death and resurrection. Grant us a foretaste of the kingdom that he will bring to consummation at his promised coming. And give us courage and hope for the service to which he has called us. We pray in his name, Amen.[1]

Martha: I have to admit that I just don't get much out of the Lord's Supper. To me, it just seems like an empty ritual.

Jerry: I love Communion Sundays. It's the one time when we really seem to come together as a church family and where everyone is welcome and included, regardless of background or belief.

Lisa: I know that Catholics believe that the bread and wine become Jesus' body and blood. But for us the bread and wine are just symbols, right?

Max: But I am sometimes moved to tears when I receive the elements. Somehow Jesus really does seem close by.

1. Based on C67 9.52.

The Lord's Supper powerfully represents the unity of those who have been baptized into the death and resurrection of Jesus Christ. We eat and drink with each other and the risen Lord. But, ironically and tragically, the meal that should unite Christians has all too often divided them. Even today, Catholic and Orthodox churches prohibit their members from receiving the Lord's Supper in a Protestant church and do not offer the Eucharist to Protestants in their churches. The fact that exceptions are sometimes made does not change official Catholic and Orthodox teaching that Protestants are not fully members of the true church, which is the body of Christ, and therefore should not participate in the sacrament, which incorporates people into Christ's body. Historically, Protestants too restricted access to the Lord's Supper. John Calvin and his followers "fenced" the table, arguing that only people who were repentant of their sins could properly receive the bread and the cup. At the same time, Calvin was deeply distressed that the new Protestant churches were soon quarreling about the meaning of the Lord's Supper and who could receive it. His efforts to overcome these divisions, especially with the Lutherans, ultimately failed.

Today the situation is different. Many Protestant churches practice an "open table." All people baptized in the name of the Father, and the Son, and the Holy Spirit—regardless of their denominational affiliation or spiritual state—are welcome to receive communion. There has also been a growing desire in many churches to invite people who, though not yet baptized, are nevertheless seeking Christ and participating in the community of faith.[2] Some church leaders go so far as to say that the Lord's Supper should be open even to members of other religions or people of no religion at all who nevertheless wish to participate. From this perspective, the table should be a place of inclusion, where we represent our commitment to honor each other as God's children, without respect to our different backgrounds and social identities. To exclude anyone from the table would be not only bad hospitality but also an assault on their dignity.

2. In 2016, the General Assembly of the Presbyterian Church (U.S.A.) made changes to its *Directory for Worship* to affirm this stance. See W-3.0409.

This spirit of practical ecumenical cooperation has not, however, resolved the question of just how God is at work in the Lord's Supper. Catholic, Orthodox, and some Protestant traditions speak of Christ's "real presence" in the Supper but have different ways of understanding how he is present and whether the bread and the wine are somehow transformed into his body and blood. For other traditions, such as Baptist, communion, like baptism, is an "ordinance," not a sacrament. For them, Christ ordained this meal to remind us of his Last Supper, when he prepared to go to the cross for our salvation. Moreover, people, regardless of theological tradition, experience communion in vastly different ways. Some people feel deep emotions, while for others it is an empty ritual. Some want to receive the sacrament weekly, while others say that it will be more special if the church celebrates it less frequently.

Every congregation under the guidance of its pastor and session must make practical decisions about what words to use in the eucharistic prayers, the manner in which to serve the bread and the cup, and how often to celebrate the meal. The confessions will not answer all of these questions for us, but they will help us better understand what kind of an event the Lord's Supper is, so that our way of observing it will better correspond to what we believe about how God is at work there.

The confessions have similar understandings of preaching, baptism, and the Lord's Supper. All three events are external means of grace by which God acts through his Holy Spirit to draw us more deeply into the life of the risen Christ. While preaching relies on words alone, baptism and the Lord's Supper use materials things — water, bread, and wine — together with words to impress the promises of God more deeply upon us. The sacraments are not essential to salvation; what matters ultimately is the faith that comes directly from God. Nevertheless, those who have faith will regard the sacraments as good gifts from God for strengthening their faith and for impelling them to live it out more fully in acts of love and mercy within the covenant community and beyond. Thus the sacraments relate us both to God and to each other as members of the body of Christ commissioned to witness to God's ways in the world.

We gain some clues to the meaning of the Lord's Supper from the different names that it has received over the centuries. In the ancient church, the sacrament was known as the Eucharist, from the Greek word for thanksgiving, because in celebrating the sacrament the church lifted up prayers of thanksgiving for Christ's saving work in his death and resurrection. In traditional Roman Catholicism, the Lord's Supper was sometimes referred to as the Mass or the canon of the Mass, as though the entire point of the worship service (the Mass) was to celebrate the sacrament. Eastern Orthodoxy has spoken of the *anaphora*, from the Greek for "offering up," in reference both to the prayers that the church offers up and to Christ's offering up of himself. Anabaptist churches have sometimes called the Supper simply "the breaking of the bread." Luther used a variety of terms, including the "sacrament of the altar." Reformed churches have preferred "Lord's Supper" or "Communion." For them, the sacrament is celebrated as a meal and, moreover, as a community meal. Whereas in the Catholic Church a priest can celebrate the Mass all alone, in Reformed understanding the members of the congregation eat the Lord's Supper together.

The Scots Confession speaks of the "Supper or Table of the Lord Jesus, also called the Communion of His Body and Blood" (SC 3.21). The Heidelberg Catechism refers to the "Holy Supper" or the "Lord's Supper" (HC 4.075 and 4.077). The Second Helvetic Confession, the Westminster Confession of Faith, and the Confession of 1967 also favor the term Lord's Supper (SH 5.193; WC 6.161; and C67 9.52). Because the Supper is a meal, the Reformed tradition has not spoken of an "altar" for a sacrifice, but rather of a "table" at which Christ's followers gather. In the Scottish Presbyterian tradition, churches actually set up tables in the sanctuary on a Communion Sunday, and people passed the bread and the cup to each other; some Presbyterian churches in the United States continued this practice into the early twentieth century. People did not simply look at the bread and the wine from afar and revere or adore them, as often happened in medieval Catholicism. Rather, they ate and shared fellowship at this special meal, just as they might at other meals.

The confessions attach promises of God to this communal eating of bread and wine. The Reformation-era confessions agree that the Supper sets forth, first, God's promise of *forgiveness*. For the Heidelberg Catechism, "to eat the crucified body of Christ and to drink his poured-out blood . . . [means] to receive forgiveness of sins" (HC 4.076). The Second Helvetic Confession declares that "by having given his body and shed his blood [Christ] has pardoned all our sins" (SH 5.195). The Confession of 1967, in accord with its theme of reconciliation, sees the Lord's Supper as "a celebration of the reconciliation of men with God" (C67 9.52).

Second, the act of eating bread and drinking wine dramatizes God's promise to *nourish* us in faith. Just as we take bread into our bodies to "strengthen" ourselves and drink to "refresh" ourselves, so too, says the Scots Confession, "in the Supper rightly used, Christ Jesus is so joined with us that he becomes the very nourishment and food of our souls" (SC 3.21). The Heidelberg Catechism declares that "as surely as I . . . taste with my mouth the bread and cup, . . . [Christ] nourishes and refreshes my soul" (HC 4.075). According to the Second Helvetic Confession, "even as bodily food and drink not only refresh and strengthen our bodies, but also keep them alive, so the flesh of Christ delivered for us, and his blood shed for us, not only refresh and strengthen our souls, but also preserve them alive" (SH 5.199). Christ so "feeds us" and "nourishes us" (SH 5.195) that he "lives in us, and we live in him" (SH 5.198). The Westminster Confession of Faith speaks of the "spiritual nourishment" and "communion with [Christ]" that the Supper provides (WC 6.161).

The twentieth-century confessions reaffirm these themes. The Confession of 1967 says that believers are "partaking in [Christ] as they eat the bread and drink the cup" (C67 9.52). A Brief Statement of Faith tells us that the Spirit "feeds us with the bread of life and the cup of salvation" (BSF #63). "Nourishing," "refreshing," and "feeding"—these very physical dimensions of the ordinary meals that people eat together help point us to the special spiritual meanings of the Lord's Supper.

As with baptism, the confessions leave unresolved just how the Lord's Supper represents the living, resurrected Christ to us: Is the Supper primarily a memorial meal (see SH 5.195)? Does an intensive remembering of Christ's sacrifice allow us to experience the sacrament's benefits? Or are two processes taking place parallel to each other when we receive the sacrament? As we consume the Supper's bread and wine physically and outwardly, is the Spirit simultaneously feeding us spiritually and inwardly (see HC 4.075; SH 5.196; and WC 6.167)? Alternatively, does God somehow use the bread and the wine to transmit Christ's very presence to us in a special way, as John Calvin believed? For him, the Supper does not merely remind us of, or point us to, God's spiritual nourishment and refreshment. Rather, when we partake of the bread and the cup, we truly encounter the risen, living Christ. Among the confessions, the Scots Confession comes closest to this position, while carefully distinguishing itself from traditional Roman Catholic teaching about the "real presence" of Christ in the sacrament (SC 3.21).

In the late Middle Ages, Catholic theologians such as Thomas Aquinas developed the idea that the priest's consecration of the bread and wine at the altar brings about their "transubstantiation" into the body and blood of Christ. "Transubstantiation" draws on philosophical categories of the ancient Greek philosopher Aristotle, for whom every material thing is composed of a "substance" and its "accidents" (what we would call its external qualities or attributes). A piece of wood has a wooden substance that we experience as having particular "accidents": the wood is hard or soft, finely or coarsely grained, and dark or light in color. The "accidents" may vary from one piece of wood to another, but all of them have the same wood "substance." In the same way, bread and wine are substances to which particular accidents adhere. By the action of the priest, these substances are changed, while the accidents of bread and wine remain. The bread (or wine) looks and tastes like bread (or wine) but in substance is now the body (or blood) of Christ. We receive Christ's spiritual power by receiving his transfigured resurrection body into our bodies.

The confessions strongly reject transubstantiation: We do not "imagine any transubstantiation of bread into Christ's body, and of wine into his natural blood" (SC 3.21); "the holy bread of the Lord's Supper does not become the actual body of Christ" (HC

4.078; see also 4.080); "we do not . . . say that the bread itself is the body of Christ except in a sacramental way" (SH 5.205); and "the outward elements . . . in substance and nature . . . still remain truly, and only, bread and wine, as they were before" (WC 6.165). The confessions base their argument, in part, on the idea, shared by Calvin, that Christ's resurrection body has a specific location; it is in "heaven" and therefore cannot be on the altar (see HC 4.076 and SH 5.205). What is more important, however, is their affirmation that we truly experience Christ's presence when we receive the sacrament.

The Scots Confession, like Calvin, is clear that although the bread remains bread and the wine remains wine, the Holy Spirit uses our partaking of this bread and wine to carry "us above all things that are visible, carnal, and earthly, and . . . [to feed us] upon the body and blood of Christ Jesus, once broken and shed for us but now in heaven, and appearing for us in the presence of his Father" (SC 3.21; see also SH 5.205). Moreover, the confession has especially rich language for the mysterious union that the sacrament brings about with Christ's resurrection body: "We confess and believe without doubt that the faithful, in the right use of the Lord's Table, do so eat the body and drink the blood of the Lord Jesus that he remains in them and they in him; they are so made flesh of his flesh and bone of his bone that as the eternal Godhood has given to the flesh of Christ, which by nature was corruptible and mortal, life and immortality, so the eating and drinking of the flesh and blood of Christ Jesus does the like for us" (SC 3.21). So too, the Heidelberg Catechism declares that "through the Holy Spirit . . . we are united more and more to Christ's blessed body; . . . we are flesh of his flesh and bone of his bone" (HC 4.076).

Regardless of how the sacrament brings us to Christ (whether by remembrance, spiritual feeding, or lifting us up to his presence in heaven), the confessions agree that in the end the Supper offers us, as the Scots Confession declares, "immortality." According to the Heidelberg Catechism, in the sacrament we "receive forgiveness of sins and eternal life" (HC 4.076). The Second Helvetic

Confession tells us that we are "nourished unto life eternal" (SH 5.196). The Confession of 1967, while not speaking of eternal life, reminds us that the sacrament promises the ultimate transformation of all reality: at the Supper, "we rejoice in the foretaste of the kingdom which [Christ] will bring to consummation at his promised coming" (C67 9.52).

The confessions offer two qualifications, however. First, the life that we have in Christ is not yet complete. Our "immortality" is glimpsed and anticipated, but we still struggle with sin and often succumb to sin. As we saw with justification and sanctification, Christians live in the paradoxical situation of the "already/not yet." Our salvation is already assured, yet we are still growing in faith. Both baptism and the Lord's Supper set forth this paradox. Baptism is once and for all, yet we must remind ourselves daily of our new identity in Christ and grow more fully into it. The Lord's Supper sets forth Christ's one and only death for our salvation, yet we must receive the bread and wine again and again, as nourishment for our life in Christ. As the Second Helvetic Confession states, "When [a Christian] now receives the Sacrament, . . . he progresses in continuing to communicate in the body and blood of the Lord, and so his faith is kindled and grows more and more" (SH 5.203). The Westminster Larger Catechism tells us that the Supper is for "our growth in faith" (WLC 7.278).

The eternal life that the sacrament offers us is qualified, second, by our failure to experience fully what is happening when we commune. As the Scots Confession notes, "The faithful, hindered by negligence and human weakness, do not profit as much as they ought in the actual moment of the Supper" (SC 3.21). Nevertheless, despite our dullness, a deeper union with Christ does take place, and "afterwards it shall bring forth fruit, being living seed sown in good ground, for the Holy Spirit . . . will not deprive the faithful of the fruit of that mystical action" (SC 3.21).

The confessions declare that it is the Holy Spirit, not our personal worthiness or efforts, that makes the sacrament effectual for our salvation. They also emphasize that the act of receiving the bread and wine does not automatically give us God's grace.

While the Supper is for people whose faith is weak, we must have some faith in Christ, by the power of the Spirit, if the sacrament is to benefit us (see SH 5.200). We will be able to grow more fully into the life of Christ only if we first know and affirm that we belong, however imperfectly, to him and his body, the community of faith—which explains why Reformed churches have traditionally reserved communion for the baptized.

As the sacrament strengthens our communion with Christ, it also moves us to reach out to others within and beyond the community of faith. According to the Second Helvetic Confession, "We are admonished in the celebration of the Supper of the Lord to be mindful of whose body we have become members, and that, therefore, we may be of one mind with the brethren [and] live a holy life" (SH 5.207). For the Westminster Confession of Faith, the Supper is a "bond and pledge" of our communion not only with Christ but also "with each other, as members of his mystical body" (WC 6.161). The Confession of 1967 adds that the sacrament gives us "courage and hope for the service to which [Christ] has called [us]," the ministry of reconciliation (C67 9.52). Our mystical union with Christ leads to the hard work of living more fully in his ways.

While the sacrament thus has implications for Christian ethics, it is equally true that how we behave has implications for the sacrament. According to the confessions, we will participate in the Supper rightly only if we are demonstrating a commitment to living in Christ's ways, no matter how far we fall short. As the Scots Confession states, "Those who eat and drink at that holy table without faith, or without peace and goodwill to their brethren, eat unworthily" (SC 3.23). The Second Helvetic Confession tells us that before we come to the sacrament, we should examine whether we are "determined to change [our] wicked life . . . and with the Lord's help to persevere in the true religion and in harmony with the brethren" (SH 5.207).

In traditional Reformed practice, the pastor and the elders visited members of the congregation prior to a Communion Sunday in order to encourage and evaluate people's self-examination and repentance (see SC 3.23). The Heidelberg Catechism states that "according to the instruction of Christ and his apostles, the Christian church is duty-bound to exclude" from the Supper those "who show by what they profess and how they live that they are unbelieving and ungodly . . . until they reform their lives" (HC 4.082).

Today, such practices may strike us as excessively legalistic and judgmental. Who is any of us to determine whether others should be excluded from the table, when all of us come to it as sinners? Nevertheless, the confessions have a helpful insight here. The Supper will benefit us only to the degree that we know how much we need it. The Heidelberg Catechism forcefully states that only those should come to the table "who are displeased with themselves because of their sins, but who nevertheless trust that their sins are pardoned and that their remaining weakness is covered by the suffering and death of Christ, and who also desire more and more to strengthen their faith, and to lead a better life. Hypocrites and those who are unrepentant, however, eat and drink judgment on themselves" (HC 4.081; see also SH 5.207). We will honor the sacrament only if we are seeking with repentant hearts to trust God and serve others.

The idea of mystically communing directly with Christ, so central to the Reformation-era understanding of the Lord's Supper, does not make sense to many people today. "Being lifted up to heaven" or "being fed the body of Christ" may strike us as beautiful metaphors, but not what we literally experience at the time of communion. We may understand how the Lord's Supper commits us to each other and calls us into a Christian way of life, but how the bread and cup communicate Christ's eternal life to us is more elusive. The Confession of 1967 comes perhaps closest to what meaningful communion is for many church members today: a means of "equipping" us to serve the world (C67 9.48). In dramatic form the Supper represents the reconciliation among people for which God calls us to work in all of our relationships (see C67 9.43).

Nevertheless, the confessions make clear that reconciliation among humans flows out of the reconciliation that God has first offered us in Jesus Christ. To be fully human is to know that our life is a good gift from a creating and redeeming God who wants us to live in freedom before him and with others, rather than in bondage to any lesser, worldly power. The sacrament teaches us that reconciliation among humans is more than a matter of getting along with each other and respecting each other, although reconciliation certainly includes cooperation and respect. Reconciliation is, first of all, life together before God; it expresses itself as worship, where we praise God, confess our sins before God, call on God to forgive and renew us, offer God thanks for his justifying and sanctifying work in Christ, and recommit ourselves to God's ways as revealed in Christ.

The confessions leave open the practical question of how best to shape our celebrations of the Lord's Supper so that they will correspond to its deepest spiritual meanings. But the confessions' confidence that Christ truly meets us in the sacrament—whether we are aware of him or not, whether we immediately benefit from the Supper or not—suggests several key considerations.

For one thing, celebration of the Lord's Supper will be frequent enough to represent our continuous need for Christ's spiritual nourishment yet infrequent enough to provide time for self-examination and recognition of our hunger for Christ. For another, the prayers of the eucharistic liturgy will focus less on our intentions to be a welcoming, inclusive community (as important as these commitments are) and more on God's promises to us in Jesus Christ: forgiveness of sin, strength through his Holy Spirit to die to the old life of sin so that we may live for God and others, and renewed communion with the Creator, who is our Redeemer. In addition, the tone of the service will be joyful yet solemn; next to our wondrous glimpsing of God's new heaven and earth will be a chastened recognition of how far we still fall short of being the new creation that is our true identity in Jesus Christ. And the bread and the cup will be displayed and served in a way that draws our attention to the Supper as a community meal that not only feeds us individually but also calls us into deeper love and care for each other.

However we celebrate the Lord's Supper, we do so in the humble awareness that we will never exhaust its meaning. It will be our teacher all of our lives, for it offers us the Teacher, Jesus Christ, present to us always in the power of the Holy Spirit.

FOR DISCUSSION

Concerns Raised in the Opening Dialogue

Is the Lord's Supper just an empty ritual?

Is communion primarily about celebrating community with each other?

Are the bread and cup just symbols, or do they somehow become the body and blood of Christ?

Does Christ come closer to us through the Lord's Supper?

Questions

1. The confessions speak of the Lord's Supper as remembrance, spiritual feeding, and mystical communion with Christ in heaven. Which of these meanings do you think is most important to people in your congregation? Why?
2. What could a congregation do to prepare itself better for receiving the Lord's Supper?
3. Look again at the last two paragraphs of this chapter. Which suggestions could be helpful for your congregation?
4. How would you explain the significance of the Lord's Supper for living out our faith in the world?

CHAPTER 11

FACING DEATH

Opening Prayer: God of mercy and justice, you call us to be the salt of the earth and the light of the world, and to witness by word and deed to your new heaven and earth, which we have already received in Jesus Christ. Bring us to a new obedience that opens up new possibilities of life for society and the world. May thy kingdom come, and may we faithfully represent it. Amen.[1]

Martha: I wonder how our church can better reach out to people who are dying or who have recently experienced the death of a loved one.

Jerry: Well, I don't think that we can necessarily promise heaven to them. There's just too much we don't know about who really belongs to God and who doesn't.

Lisa: But it seems to me that the promises of God are for all people. Every funeral service in our sanctuary is an opportunity for us to proclaim God's victory over sin and death through the resurrection of his Son.

Max: It really bothers me when a funeral service focuses so much on who the deceased was. How can a funeral

---

1. Based on CB 10.5.

service help us see that God is bringing peace and justice to the whole creation?

At the heart of the Christian faith lies the conviction that Jesus has been raised from the dead. When some Christians in ancient Corinth denied the resurrection, the apostle Paul sharply rebuked them: "If there is no resurrection of the dead, then Christ has not been raised; and if Christ has not been raised, then our proclamation has been in vain and your faith has been in vain" (1 Cor. 15:13–14). Each of the Gospels concludes with women coming to Jesus' tomb and finding it empty, because "he has been raised"; several Gospels also record appearances of the resurrected Christ to his male disciples. For the first Christians, Easter was the most important day of the year, and they regarded every Sunday as a further celebration of Jesus' resurrection.

Christ's victory over death is the basis of the Christian hope that God will also care for each of us in death — and beyond death. In words that are often read at funeral services, Paul proclaims that "neither death, nor life, nor angels, nor rulers, nor things present, nor things to come, nor powers, nor height, nor depth, nor anything else in all creation, will be able to separate us from the love of God in Christ Jesus our Lord" (Rom. 8:38). The Gospel of John speaks of life in Christ as "eternal life" (see John 3:15). The ancient creeds conclude with affirmations that our life with God does not cease when we die. The Nicene Creed declares that "we look for the resurrection of the dead, and the life of the world to come" (NC 1.3). In the Apostles' Creed, we confess "the resurrection of the body; and the life everlasting" (AC 2.3).

One of the most profound opportunities for the church to proclaim its Easter faith is at the time of a funeral, which the Presbyterian *Book of Common Worship* calls "a service of witness to the resurrection." Death occurs under many different circumstances, and our reactions to it can range from shock and disbelief when someone dies too early in life as a result of an accident or incurable disease, to acceptance and even relief when someone has lived with chronic pain or crippling disability for many years. But regardless of how "good" or "bad" a particular death seems, we long to know that death does not have the last word. At a funeral, we ache for comfort in the wake of grief and loss, for assurance that God is truly with us despite the unknown, and for renewed strength for the work that God has given us to do until we too must die.

The confessions explore these themes by examining not only the fate of the individual after death but also the consummation of all of history, when God's victory over every manifestation of sin and death will be complete. Even now, we live in the confidence that God is directing our lives and human events around us. What happens to us personally cannot be separated from what God is doing to redeem the whole of creation. Our faith in God's ultimate purposes at the end of time makes it possible for us to face life and death with courage here and now.

In earlier chapters, we spoke of how God created humans for communion with him, with each other, and with the creation. Our lives should therefore be characterized by awe at, and gratitude for, life as a free and wondrous gift of God. We should trust in God, certain that the One who created us also sustains us and cares for us in the midst of life's everyday problems and difficulties. God makes it possible for us to know him—to enter into his life, which is truth and goodness. Through Christ, all that separates us from God and each other has been overcome. As a "new creation" (2 Cor. 5:17), we dedicate ourselves to serving others so that they might know that they too belong to God.

But death easily calls all of these hopes into question. Joy and wonder in human existence no longer seem possible. The good that we have been privileged to know now appears fragile and uncertain. In the face of death, everything that we have cared about and given our lives to seems to be taken away. We may wonder whether there is really a God, or whether we have simply made up a fantasy. We easily become anxious, uncertain of the worth and meaning of our lives.

The Reformation-era confessions assure us that death does not mean the end of our life in Christ. On the contrary—and perhaps to our great surprise—death, according to the confessions, actually leads believers into even more perfect communion with God.

In explicating this point, the confessions lay out a series of events that transpire from the time of a person's death until Christ's second coming. Both "soul" and "body" participate in these events. Neither is lost to God, and both are subject to Christ's judgment and redemption at the end of time. We must be careful, however, not to take these descriptions too literally. The confessions are speaking of realities that go beyond what we can know or experience in this world and therefore for which we finally have no words. The confessions give us a collage of inexact images, some of which may seem very strange to us, even as they convey truths by which we can live.

According to the confessions, the soul is an immortal substance that does not disappear or fall "asleep" at the time of one's death (see SC 3.17 and WC 6.177). Rather, the soul separates from the body, returns to God, and enters into the condition ("heaven" or "hell") that corresponds to its status as "saved" or "damned." The Scots Confession teaches that upon death the souls of believers "are delivered from all fear and torment, and all the temptations to which we and all God's chosen are subject in this life," while "the reprobate and unfaithful departed have anguish, torment, and pain which cannot be expressed" (SC 3.17). The Westminster Confession of Faith says that "the souls of the righteous, being then made perfect in holiness, are received into the highest heavens, where they behold the face of God in light and glory, . . . [but] the souls of the wicked are cast into hell, where they remain in torments and utter darkness" (WC 6.177); the confessions reject the possibility that souls could go to a third place, such as purgatory (see WC 6.177 and SH 5.238), where, according to Catholic thinking, sinful souls can purify themselves and can, after many thousands of years, become fit for heaven.

While the soul is in heaven or hell, the body decays and returns to dust (WC 6.177). But even in the grave, the body, like the soul, is somehow experiencing "heaven" or "hell." According to the Westminster Larger Catechism, the bodies of believers remain "united to Christ" and "rest in their graves as in their beds," while the bodies of the wicked are "kept in their graves, as in their prisons" (WLC 7.196). These parallel conditions of body and soul suggest that while body and soul can be distinguished, they belong together; the fate of one is also the fate of the other. The confessions do not regard the soul as more important or more essential than the body for human identity. Rather, we are truly human only as a unity of body and soul.

This emphasis on the necessary unity of body and soul is also present in the confessions' understanding of resurrection. Even though, immediately after death, the soul (and, in a different way, the body) already experiences heaven or hell, the souls of believers are nevertheless "waiting for the full redemption of their bodies" (WC 6.177). The soul's experience of heaven or hell is somehow incomplete until it is joined again to its body raised from the dead. According to the confessions, the body that a person receives in the resurrection is truly their own body, the same body that they had on earth. The Scots Confession declares that "the dead shall arise incorruptible, and in the very substance of the selfsame flesh which every man now bears, to receive . . . glory or punishment" (SC 3.25). The Heidelberg Catechism assures believers that "not only will my soul be taken immediately after this life to Christ its head, but also my very flesh will be raised by the power of Christ, reunited with my soul, and made like Christ's glorious body" (HC 4.057). In a similar manner, the Westminster Confession of Faith affirms that at the last day "all the dead shall be raised up with the selfsame bodies, and . . . shall be reunited again to their souls" (WC 6.178). In death and resurrection, we retain the unique identity that God created for each of us.

Again, however, the confessions are saying more than humans know how to say about the ultimate purposes of God. By faith we are certain that death cannot rob us of our individual existence; nevertheless, the resurrection body that is identical to our earthly body is also different from it. Jesus had the same body after his resurrection — he was not a ghost but rather had the wounds of the cross in his hands and feet (Luke 24:36–39) — yet this body could pass through closed doors (John 20:26). It was the same Jesus, yet people often had difficulty recognizing him. Mary Magdalene mistakes him for the gardener until he calls her by name (John 20:14–16), and the disciples on the road to Emmaus recognize him only after he breaks the bread and vanishes from their sight (Luke 24:31). As with Christ, our resurrection bodies are also the "self-same" yet "with different qualities" (WC 6.178). This paradoxical language points to the mystery of the resurrection even while assuring us of its reality.

According to the Reformation-era confessions, the resurrection of the body and its reunion with the soul take place at the end of time. Drawing on the Scriptures, the confessions foresee a day of judgment, when Christ will appear in glory to judge the living and the dead. The Scots Confession declares that "the same Lord Jesus shall visibly return for this Last Judgment as he was seen to ascend" (SC 3.11). According to the Second Helvetic Confession, on that day "the dead will rise again (1 Thess. 4:14 ff.) and those who on that day (which is unknown to all creatures [Mark 13:32]) will be alive will be changed 'in the twinkling of an eye,' and all the faithful will be caught up to meet Christ in the air" (SH 5.074). These events will occur "when wickedness will then be at its greatest in the world and when the Antichrist, having corrupted true religion, will fill up all things with superstition and impiety and will cruelly lay waste the Church with bloodshed and flames" (SH 5.074), although the Westminster Confession of Faith warns us that we must "always be watchful, because [we] know not at what hour the Lord will come" (WC 6.182).

Debate has regularly arisen in church history about how to interpret Scripture's reference to a thousand-year period (millennium), when the saints will be resurrected and will rule with Christ prior to the general resurrection and the Last Judgment (see Rev. 20:4). Those who take a "premillennial" position have argued that Christ's second coming will initiate this millennium. Those who are "postmillennial" assert, in contrast, that this thousand years refers to a period in which the resurrected Christ is active in the church, as it converts people to the gospel *prior to* his second coming. Still other theologians have been "amillennial," seeing the millennium as metaphorical, not literal. In the late nineteenth century, the English clergyman John Darby promoted premillennialism through a view known as dispensationalism, which was then adopted by an American minister, Cyrus Scofield, and incorporated into his influential *Scofield Reference Bible*, first published in 1909. Dispensationalist millenarianism was popularized again in the 1970 book *The Late, Great Planet Earth* and in the late 1990s by the Left Behind series.

While the confessions pay little direct attention to the millennium, the Reformed tradition has generally worried that premillennialism encourages unhelpful speculation about the exact timing of events at the end of history, as when *The Late, Great Planet Earth* asserted that the Cold War confrontation between the United States and the Soviet Union was a fulfillment of biblical prophecy. Among the confessions, the Second Helvetic Confession is most direct in its rejection of premillennialism: "We further condemn . . . dreams that there will be a golden age on earth before the Day of Judgment, and that the pious, having subdued all their godless enemies, will possess all the kingdoms of the earth" (SH 5.075). And the Confession of 1967 clearly takes an amillennial position when it calls the kingdom "an image . . . [that] represents the triumph of God over all that resists his will and disrupts his creation" (C67 9.54).

The Reformation-era confessions declare that people at the Last Judgment will be judged "according to their works" (SC 3.25; see also WC 6.180). While the confessions' attention to works is faithful to the vision of the Last Judgment offered in the book of Revelation 20:13, it nevertheless stands in tension with the Reformation principle of "by faith alone" that the confessions otherwise affirm—and this tension should remind us yet again that the confessions (and the Scriptures) are speaking about matters for which human language and concepts end up in using paradox and acknowledging the mystery of God's ways.

At the Last Judgment, people, now in bodies resurrected from the dead, will be separated into two groups, as were their souls directly after death. The first group consists of the saints, to whom Christ gives "everlasting life" (WC 6.181), "blessed immortality" (SC 3.11), and "the fullness of joy and refreshing which . . . come from the presence of the Lord" (WC 6.181). In the words of the

Heidelberg Catechism, "After this life I will have perfect blessedness, such as no eye has seen, no ear has heard, no human heart has ever imagined; a blessedness in which to praise God forever" (HC 4.058).

The Westminster documents emphasize that believers will be freed "from all sin and misery" (WLC 7.200) and will be "made perfectly holy and happy both in body and soul" (WLC 7.200). In the words of the Westminster Shorter Catechism, they will enjoy "God to all eternity" (WSC 7.038, an allusion to the catechism's opening affirmation that "man's chief end is . . . to enjoy [God] forever" [WSC 7.001]). The saints will reign eternally with Christ (SC 3.25) and, according to the Westminster Larger Catechism, will join him "in the judging of reprobate angels and men" (WLC 7.200). Moreover, those who belong to Christ will receive and do all of these things together, along with "the company of innumerable saints and angels" (WLC 7.200), and in bodies now conformed to Christ's glorious body (see SC 3.25; HC 4.057; and WC 6.179).

At the Last Judgment, the reprobate experience a fate in every way opposite to that of the saints. The Heidelberg Catechism warns us that "no unchaste person, no idolater, adulterer, thief, no covetous person, no drunkard, slanderer, robber, or the like will inherit the kingdom of God" (HC 4.087). According to the Scots Confession, "the stubborn, disobedient, cruel persecutors, filthy persons, idolaters, and all sorts of the unbelieving, shall be cast into the dungeon of utter darkness, where their worm shall not die, nor their fire be quenched" (a reference to Mark 9:48) (SC 3.11); they "shall be tormented forever, both in body and in spirit" (SC 3.25). The Second Helvetic Confession declares that "unbelievers and the ungodly will descend with the devils into hell to burn forever and never to be redeemed from torments (Matt. 25:46)" (SH 5.074; see also WLC 7.199). Their bodies have been raised not to glory, but rather to "dishonor" (WC 6.179; see also WLC 7.197).

At first glance, we may find ourselves confused about the reason for a Last Judgment, given that believers and unbelievers have already been judged, separated, and assigned to their different destinies at the moment of death. It is not immediately obvious how the fate of the person reunited as body and soul differs from their previous enjoyment of heaven or suffering in hell as a soul without a body. But, as we have seen, the Reformation-era confessions regard humans as fully human only as body and soul together. The confessions suggest that the joys of heaven or the torments of hell are all the more intense when not the soul alone but rather the soul and the body together experience them. According to the Westminster Larger Catechism, the communion with Christ that believers already experience upon death is "at last perfected at the resurrection and the day of judgment" (WLC 7.192). To the glories that the soul experiences apart from the body is added, after the resurrection of the body, "the immediate vision and fruition of God the Father, of our Lord Jesus Christ, and of the Holy Spirit to all eternity" (WLC 7.200).

The Westminster documents use an especially arresting image for the fate of the reprobate after the Last Judgment: eternal separation from God. According to the Westminster Confession of Faith, unbelievers will be "punished with everlasting destruction from the presence of the Lord, and from the glory of his power" (WC 6.181). The Westminster Larger Catechism further declares that the wicked "shall be cast out from the favorable presence of God, and the glorious fellowship with Christ, his saints, and all the holy angels" (WLC 7.199). Here again language reaches a breaking point, saying more than humans know how to say. If God is God, we will doubt that anyone can ever be entirely separated from God and his love, at least so far as God is concerned. As the Scots Confession affirms, when Christ appears in judgment and renders up the kingdom to God, then God "shall be and ever shall remain, all in all things" (a reference to 1 Cor. 15:28) (SC 3.25).

Perhaps for this reason, more recent documents in the *Book of Confessions* no longer speak of a Last Judgment that separates the saints and the reprobate, or speculate about a heaven or hell that awaits individual believers, but rather emphasize God's will to transform the whole creation. A Brief Statement of Faith compares God to "a mother who will not forsake her nursing child, . . . a father who runs to welcome the prodigal home" (BSF ##49–51). We can therefore be sure that "nothing in life or in death can separate us from the love of God in Christ Jesus our Lord" (BSF

##78–79; see Rom. 8:38–39). According to the Confession of 1967, "God's redeeming work in Jesus Christ embraces the whole of man's life. . . . It is the will of God that his purpose for human life shall be fulfilled under the rule of Christ and all evil be banished from his creation" (C67 9.53).

From another angle, however, the promise of heaven and the threat of hell remain important tenets of Christian faith because they affect how we live right now. According to the Scots Confession, our anticipation of a Last Judgment is "not only a bridle by which our carnal lusts are restrained but also such inestimable comfort that neither the threatening of worldly powers, nor the fear of present danger or of temporal death, may move us to renounce and forsake that blessed society which we . . . have with our Head and only Mediator, Christ Jesus" (SC 3.11; see also WC 6.182). Moreover, the very promise of heaven actually offers believers a glimpse of heaven here and now; in the words of the Heidelberg Catechism, "I already now experience in my heart the beginning of eternal joy" (SC 4.058). Gratitude, trust, hope, joy, and love then shape our daily existence.

The twentieth-century confessions show how the Bible's language of "the last things" makes a difference for our commitment to justice for the time that we have on earth. The Confession of 1967 declares that "already God's reign is present as a ferment in the world, stirring hope in men and preparing the world to receive its ultimate judgment and redemption" (C67 9.54). This hope gives birth to an urgency within the church to apply "itself to present tasks and [strive] for a better world" (C67 9.55). To be sure, the church cannot bring God's kingdom into reality. But when it does what it can to point to God's ways in the world, the church does not "despair in the face of disappointment and defeat . . . and looks beyond all partial achievements to the final triumph of God" (C67 9.55). The Confession of Belhar calls the church to "witness both by word and by deed to the new heaven and the new earth in which righteousness dwells" (CB 10.5). The church does so by striving "against any form of injustice, so that justice may roll down like waters, and righteousness like an ever-flowing stream" (CB 10.7). In the words of A Brief Statement of Faith, "we watch for God's new heaven and new earth," confident that God's purposes will ultimately prevail (BSF ##75–76).

Death is never far from any of us. When those whom we love die or when we contemplate our own mortality, we may experience grief, fear, and melancholy. It is for just such a people in distress that God calls the church to witness to Christ's victory over sin and death. Scripture declares that nothing can separate us from God and that God keeps seeking us out to know him and to live in communion with him. The words of the Heidelberg Catechism, which we earlier related to baptismal identity, should resound again at the time of a funeral: My "only comfort in life and in death" is "that I am not my own, but belong—body and soul, in life and in death—to my faithful Savior Jesus Christ. . . . Because I belong to him, Christ, by his Holy Spirit, assures me of eternal life and makes me wholeheartedly willing and ready from now on to live for him" (HC 4.001).

When we live by this assurance, we will not speculate about our future fate in heaven or hell, but rather will be impelled to serve God and our fellow humans on earth. Those who know that they belong to Christ want to grow in his ways and to do whatever they can to encourage goodness, justice, and peace. Faith and works need not be opposites; in Christ, faith necessarily issues in, and is strengthened by, deeds of love and gratitude. The biblical image of a day of judgment demands that we take seriously these responsibilities to Christ. But Scripture also assures us that God's judgment is God's gracious redemption. God desires that all of us come into deeper communion with him and with all that belongs to God.

FOR DISCUSSION

Concerns Raised in the Opening Dialogue

How can the church better reach out to those facing death and those affected by death?
We can't promise heaven to anyone, can we?

What is the purpose of a funeral service?

What are God's ultimate purposes for this world in which we
live?

Questions

1. How important is the body to the unique identity that God
   has given each person?
2. What can the church with integrity promise to those who are
   dying and to those who are grieving death?
3. What elements of worship do you think could help a funeral
   service truly be a witness to the resurrection?
4. What are we asking for when we pray, "Thy kingdom come"?

CHAPTER 12

THE CHURCH'S
RESPONSIBILITY TO SOCIETY

Opening Prayer: O God, in a broken and fearful world, give us courage by the power of your Spirit to pray without ceasing, to witness among all peoples to Christ as Lord and Savior, to unmask idolatries in church and culture, to hear the voices of people long silenced, and to work with others for justice, freedom, and peace, even as we watch for your new heaven and earth. Amen.[1]

Martha: I just heard that the Congress is considering a measure that would favor the wealthy and hurt the poor. We need to do something!

Jerry: I just don't think the church should get involved in politics. These issues are so complicated, and we have people in our congregation on both sides. The last thing we need is to anger someone.

Lisa: Besides, we don't have any influence on politics anyway. Wouldn't it be better for us to focus on attracting more people to our church, so that they can know the good news of Jesus Christ?

1. Based on BSF ##65–71 and 75.

Max: But the gospel calls us to reach out to the weak and oppressed. The question is not whether, but rather how.

One of the most important and yet controversial matters of contemporary church life is Christian involvement in society and politics. Over the centuries, Christians have related to the world around them in a wide variety of ways. Some Christians have called for the church to step back from society and politics to focus on its own life as a community of faith, while others have argued that Christian social and political involvement is essential to the gospel, although they have not always agreed on solutions to specific social and political problems.

The first Christians regarded themselves as "aliens and exiles" (1 Pet. 2:11) in the pagan world of the Roman Empire. Because they rejected both violent coercion and state-enforced veneration of other gods, Christians did not serve in the military or government posts. They assumed that they would face social discrimination and even persecution from the rulers, sometimes unto death. To be a Christian meant to be part of an alternative political order that was ruled by Christ rather than by the powers of this world. Christians exercised influence on society only by their example of self-giving love and mutual care. They believed that they should respect the ruler and pray for him (see 1 Pet. 2:13–14 and 1 Tim. 2:1–2), but they did not aspire to a kingship of this world.

The conversion of Emperor Constantine to Christianity in the early fourth century dramatically altered the church's lot. In the next decades, Christianity established itself as the favored religion of the Roman Empire. Christians entered fully into all areas of social and political life, including the government. A Christian civilization arose; Christian symbols, narratives, and moral values shaped the rhythms and patterns of everyday life. Political and church leaders supported each other and sometimes were the same people, such as Gregory the Great (540–604), who served as prefect (governor) of Rome before taking monastic vows and later becoming pope.

The relation of church and state was rarely harmonious, however. Political rulers often saw the church as little more than a political instrument to strengthen their authority and root out their opponents by labeling them as heretics, whereas church leaders wanted the state to secure their power through political coercion. One matter in which things came to a head concerned who had the right to appoint bishops, with the church increasingly resenting political rulers' intervention in what the church considered its internal affairs. Other historical factors further complicated church-state relations. After the eighth century, the eastern part of the empire—known as Byzantium and centered in Constantinople—came under the domination of Islam. In the West, the ideal of a Christian civilization continued to develop, reaching a highpoint in the twelfth and thirteenth centuries, but then came under pressure from various renewal movements, including the Protestant Reformation of the sixteenth century.

The splintering of Christianity after the Reformation was reflected politically. In the Thirty Years' War (1618–48), European states with rival religious identities, Catholic and Protestant, fought against each other. The widespread destruction and chaos that resulted eventually encouraged political leaders to embrace principles of religious toleration and the separation of church and state. Christians began to understand themselves as just one voice among many in national states governed by secular law. Moreover, Christians increasingly had to acknowledge that Christianity itself lent support to a wide variety of social and political positions. It became increasingly difficult to speak of *the* Christian position on social and political issues that were sometimes extremely complicated and ambiguous.

As Presbyterians and other Reformed Christians seek political guidance in our time, the *Book of Confessions* offers a biblical, theological understanding of government and the church's mission in society. The confessions help us understand what we should expect of government—and what we must not expect—as well as what kind of people Christians should be as they relate to their society. Presbyterians and other Christians will not always agree on concrete social or political policy proposals, but the confessions remind us that even when our influence is limited politically, God has called us to seek a more just society.

Cynicism about government is widespread in contemporary America, but the confessions remind us that the God who creates and redeems our lives guards them by providing for government while we sojourn on earth. A world without rules, laws, and political structures quickly descends into chaos and violence. Government is God's good gift to us, and we should give thanks for political officials and pray for them. In the words of the Declaration of Barmen, the church "acknowledges the benefit of this divine appointment in gratitude and reverence before [God]" (DB 8.22).

The Reformation-era confessions commend civil government to us, declaring that it has been instituted by God both to manifest his own glory and to provide for human well-being (see SC 3.24 and WC 6.127). For the Scots Confession, the civil powers are nothing less than "the lieutenants of God, and in their councils God himself doth sit and judge" (SC 3.24). The Second Helvetic Confession, following Romans 13:4 (KJV), calls the magistrate "the minister of God" (SH 5.258). Indeed, government is such a blessing that it "should have the chief place in the world" (SH 5.252). The Westminster Confession of Faith, holding a similar view, concludes that it is therefore "lawful for Christians to accept and execute the office of a magistrate, when called thereunto" (WC 6.128).

While lauding government, the confessions are equally clear about its responsibilities to its subjects. Several confessions apply the fifth commandment, "Honor thy father and mother," to rulers. The Second Helvetic Confession calls the ruler "a father" (SH 5.258). The Westminster Larger Catechism states that "superiors are styled 'fathers' and 'mothers' . . . to teach them in all duties towards their inferiors, like natural parents, to express love and tenderness to them" (WLC 7.235). In its section on the civil magistrate, as amended by American Presbyterians after the Revolutionary War, the Westminster Confession of Faith calls rulers "nursing fathers" (WC 6.129), an allusion to Isaiah 49:23 (KJV).

As loving parents, rulers are responsible to promote good and repress evil (SC 3.24 and WC 6.127). The Second Helvetic Confession declares that "the chief duty of the magistrate is to secure and preserve peace and public tranquility" (SH 5.253). The Westminster Confession of Faith and the Declaration of Barmen add a concern for "justice" (WC 6.128 and DB 8.22; see also SH 5.254). The Westminster Larger Catechism is especially expansive in its list of responsibilities: rulers are "to love, pray for, and bless their inferiors; to instruct, counsel, and admonish them, . . . rewarding such as do well, . . . [and] chastising such as do ill; protecting, and providing for them all things necessary for soul and body" (WLC 7.239). Moreover, the Second Helvetic Confession reminds rulers of their special responsibility to those who are weakest and most vulnerable in society: "widows, orphans, and the afflicted" (SH 5.254).

Several Reformation-era confessions enumerate the qualities of a good ruler. The Second Helvetic Confession asks rulers to govern "with good laws made according to the Word of God," to "exercise judgment by judging uprightly," and to reject bribes (SH 5.254). The Westminster Larger Catechism calls on magistrates to maintain "grave, wise, holy, and exemplary carriage [that is, behavior]" (WLC 7.239). The catechism adds that they must not dishonor themselves or lessen their authority by "unjust, undiscreet [*sic*], rigorous, or remiss behavior," such as neglecting their duties, seeking "their own glory, ease, profit, or pleasure," or "provoking [their subjects] to wrath" (WLC 7.240).

Drawing further upon the apostle Paul's words in Romans 13, the confessions affirm that God has given government a monopoly on public coercion so that it can fulfill its duties. Representative is the Westminster Confession of Faith, which states that God has "armed [the magistrates] with the power of the sword, for the defense and encouragement of them that are good, and for the punishment of evildoers" (WC 6.127; see also HC 4.105). Similarly, the Declaration of Barmen affirms that government relies on "the threat and exercise of force" in order to fulfill its God-given commission to secure peace and justice (DB 8.22). According to the Second Helvetic Confession, the government's use of power extends to waging war, "if [war is] necessary to preserve the safety of the people, . . . provided that [the ruler] has first sought peace by all means possible, and cannot save his people in any other way" (SH 5.256). Similarly, the Westminster Confession of Faith affirms that magistrates may lawfully "wage war upon just and necessary occasions" (WC 6.128).

Just as rulers have divinely appointed responsibilities, so too do subjects. In the words of the Heidelberg Catechism, "It is God's will . . . that I honor, love, and be loyal to . . . all those in authority over me" (HC 4.104). The Westminster Larger Catechism asks us willingly and cheerfully to obey rulers, because they are like parents (WLC 7.235). The language of the Second Helvetic Confession is equally effusive: "Let [subjects] love [the magistrate], favor him, and pray for him as their father" (SH 5.258). Moreover, the Scots Confession warns us that "so long as princes and rulers vigilantly fulfill their office, anyone who denies them aid, counsel, or service, denies it to God" (SC 3.24). Therefore, subjects are responsible to pay their taxes gladly (SH 5.258 and WC 6.130) and even to lay down their lives in war, if the magistrate requires it (SH 5.256).

To be sure, the Reformation-era language of "rulers and subjects" and "superiors and inferiors" predates modern democracies, in which all citizens bear responsibility for governance. Few of us today regard our "rulers" as mothers and fathers with whom we share special bonds of affection. Nor do we think of them as divinely appointed. Rather, we understand our political leaders to be elected officials who have been temporarily entrusted by us, the people, to negotiate competing social interests in a way that fulfills the will of the majority of citizens while protecting the rights of those in the minority. And because we believe that people with political power are always tempted to abuse it, we value a political system with checks and balances, such as in a democracy.

Nevertheless, the Reformation-era confessions, while reflecting the political realities of their time, have continuing value because they define the basic attitudes and motivations that should guide political life in every era. Those entrusted with power are to seek the good of the people, and in so doing they depend on the people's respect and support. The confessions remind us, moreover, that both the people and their political officials ultimately stand beneath God and God's purposes for government. Political life requires that we be concerned first of all not with our own interests but rather with what is pleasing to God and good for society as a whole. Even in a secular state in which government officials need not be Christian, Christians believe that political leaders and citizens alike are beholden to standards of justice and peace that conform to God's will.

While the confessions as a whole do not explicitly favor one form of government over another, they do point in the direction of democracies with their separation of church and state, limitations on the power of the state, and active citizen involvement in providing for justice and peace. In this regard, the twentieth-century confessions both revise and clarify political impulses of the earlier confessions while providing guidance for Presbyterians and Reformed Christians in the twenty-first century.

Especially valuable is the Theological Declaration of Barmen, which carefully defines the relationship of church and state. Barmen emphasizes that the state has the task of providing for justice and peace "in the as yet unredeemed world in which the Church also exists" (DB 8.22). This reference to "the as yet unredeemed world" establishes the need for government while suggesting that government will need continuing correction and reform because it too is subject to sinful distortion. Moreover, the state, according to Barmen, will be limited in its ability to achieve justice and peace because it does its work "according to the measure of human judgment and human ability" (DB 8.22), not by divine wisdom. Therefore, we must not expect the state to resolve all human problems. It will never achieve a perfect justice and peace. The church has the responsibility continually to remind the state of God's will, and the church must resist the state whenever the state seeks "over and beyond its special commission . . . [to] become the single and totalitarian order of human life" (DB 8.22).

A concern to guard the church from state control is already evident in the Westminster Confession of Faith. The original 1647 edition warns the civil magistrate not to "assume to himself the administration of the Word and Sacraments, or the power of the Keyes of the Kingdome of Heaven" (WC 6.129, footnote). The 1788, post-Revolutionary War revision retains these words while adding a warning against state interference "in matters of faith" (WC 6.129). The commentary that follows further demonstrates an American Presbyterian concern to separate church and state.

Earlier Reformed confessions had commissioned the state to promote both tables of the Decalogue, both the first table, concerned with our duties to God (religious piety), and the second table, focused on our duties to our neighbor (social justice). The Scots Confession appeals to the example of Old Testament kings to argue that "the preservation and promotion of religion is particularly the duty of kings, princes, rulers, and magistrates. They are not only appointed for civil government but also to maintain true religion and to suppress all idolatry and superstition" (SC 3.24). Similarly, the Second Helvetic Confession calls on rulers to "suppress stubborn heretics . . . who do not cease to blaspheme the majesty of God and to trouble, and even to destroy the Church of God" (SH 5.255), as does the 1647 version of the Westminster Confession of Faith (WC 6.129, footnote). The 1647 Westminster Confession of Faith adds that the magistrate is responsible to preserve the church's unity and to maintain right church doctrine, worship, and discipline (WC 6.129, footnote).

The 1788 revision reflects the new situation in the United States. While calling on the government to protect the church (and religious expression, more generally), the confession asks the government not to give preference to one religious group over another. Rather, "all ecclesiastical persons whatever shall enjoy the full, free, and unquestioned liberty of discharging every part of their sacred functions, without violence or danger. . . . No law of any commonwealth should interfere with, let, or hinder, the due exercise thereof" (WC 6.129). It is the duty of civil magistrates to protect all of their citizens, whether "upon pretense of religion or infidelity," from "any indignity, violence, abuse, or injury" (WC 6.129).

The Declaration of Barmen further specifies how the church should use a legally protected free space in society: "The Church's commission, upon which its freedom is founded, consists in delivering the message of the free grace of God to all people in Christ's stead, and therefore in the ministry of his own Word and work through sermon and Sacrament" (DB 8.26). Just as the state must not interfere in church or religious matters, the church must not use the power of the state to coerce belief from people (see

DB 8.24). Faith occurs in freedom, not as a matter of political expediency.

In sum, church and state have different responsibilities to society. The state provides for justice and peace, however imperfectly, while the church proclaims freedom from sin and the idolatrous powers of this world. Church and state also have responsibilities to each other. The state should protect freedom of religious expression, and the church in its freedom should remind the state of its commission to establish justice and peace. Constitutional separation of church and state should not eliminate religion from the public square but rather guarantee religious communities a protected space in which to promote their values, including their commitments to justice and peace. Church and state will exist in harmony, insofar as they have different spheres of concern, but at times they will find themselves in tension and even conflict. There may even be circumstances in which the church will make a necessary witness by calling for resistance to an unjust state.

At first glance, the Reformation-era confessions, with their high regard for divinely ordained government, seem to deny the possibility of ever confronting the state with its injustices. Because rulers are like parents, we should obey and respect them, even when their personal conduct falls short. The Heidelberg Catechism asks us to be "patient with their failings—for through them God chooses to rule us" (HC 4.104). Similarly, the Westminster Larger Catechism tells us to bear with rulers' infirmities, "covering them in love," so that rulers will remain an honor to a people and their government (WLC 7.237). According to the Westminster Confession of Faith, even when the ruler is an "infidel" or a non-Christian, he deserves our honor and respect (WC 6.130).

Moreover, the Reformation-era confessions seem explicitly to rule out active or violent resistance to oppressive government. The Scots Confession asserts that "any men who conspire to rebel or overturn the civil powers, as duly established, are not merely enemies to humanity but [also] rebels against God's will" (SC 3.24). The Second Helvetic Confession condemns all "rebels, enemies of the state, [and] seditious villains" (SH 5.259), while the Westminster Larger Catechism warns against cursing and mocking the rulers, let alone rebelling against them (WLC 7.238). For these confessions, government is such a precious gift to humanity that an unjust government seems better than no government at all.

Nevertheless, the Reformation-era confessions also strike a note of caution. The Second Helvetic Confession acknowledges that if the magistrate "is a friend and even a member of the Church, he is a most useful and excellent member of it, who is able to benefit it best of all," but if he "is opposed to the Church, he can hinder and disturb it very much" (SH 5.252). In delineating the responsibilities of government and the qualities of a good ruler, the confessions establish criteria for judging when a particular political order or ruler is unjust and must be resisted. While the confessions consistently call for obedience to political authority, they are also clear that obedience is warranted only so long as the rulers' commands are just, fair, and lawful (SH 5.258 and WC 6.130) and not contrary to the Word of God (SC 3.14). Otherwise, as the Scots Confession declares, Christians are "to repress tyranny [and] to defend the oppressed" (SC 3.14). Obedience to God's Word precedes obedience to any human authority (see SC 3.01 and DB 8.12; 8.22; and 8.27).

Only the more recent confessions, however, envisage the possibilities of democratic forms of government, in which Christians are citizens who have a responsibility to help shape government policies. The Declaration of Barmen, a compromise statement between those German church leaders who wished to emphasize Christian obedience to government and those who called for challenging the Nazi regime, only hints at these possibilities, when it speaks of "the responsibility both of rulers and of the ruled" to "God's commandment and righteousness" (DB 8.22). The Confession of 1967, however, is explicit about the church's duty to speak out about social and political issues: "In each time and place, there are particular problems and crises through which God calls the church to act" (C67 9.43).

According to the Confession of 1967, the reconciliation that Christ has brought about between God and humanity gives the church a distinctive commitment to human reconciliation in relation to four major issues in contemporary social and political life: racial relations and the problem of racism, international relations and the threat of nuclear war, economic relations and the scandal of poverty, and relations between men and women and the problem of the distortion of sexuality (C67 9.44–47).

The Confession of Belhar also draws on the theme of Christian reconciliation in relation not only to apartheid and racial segregation in South African church and society in the 1980s (see CB 10.5), but also more broadly to "people in any form of suffering and need" (CB 10.7). Moreover, "the church is called to confess and to do all these things, even though the authorities and human laws might forbid them and punishment and suffering be the consequence" (CB 10.9).

A Brief Statement of Faith addresses Christian responsibility for social and political issues by appealing to the work of the Holy Spirit, which "in a broken and fearful world . . . gives us courage . . . to work with others for justice, freedom, and peace" (BSF #71). A Brief Statement identifies two specific responsibilities for church involvement: "to unmask idolatries in Church and culture, [and] to hear the voices of peoples long silenced" (BSF #69-70), both of which may place the church in opposition to established and privileged powers both within its own life and in the wider society.

Unlike those Christian traditions that have called Christians to withdraw from worldly affairs, Presbyterians and the Reformed tradition have asserted that God works through political structures to bring about greater justice and peace for humanity. Just how Christians engage these matters will depend on their specific circumstances; the possibilities for political involvement in monarchies will obviously differ from those in democracies. However, the Reformed emphasis on holding every form of government responsible to God's standards of justice and peace does suggest the value of vigorous democracies that limit the power of the state and offer the church a legally protected space in which to make its witness.

The confessions emphasize that our trust in God as the supreme ruler gives us the courage to confront oppressive social and political powers, to stand by those who suffer beneath them, and to demand that the state fulfill its responsibilities to all of its citizens, including the socially weak and marginalized. From this point of view, Christian social political involvement flows directly from the church's trust in God's reconciling power in Jesus Christ, who, despite the limited progress that we see in relation to peace and justice on earth, is guiding history to its fulfillment.

Perhaps the greatest temptation for North American Presbyterians today is not social or political passivity, but rather an activism that is shaped more by secular political positions and ideologies than by the Word of God. Only a renewed commitment to responding to God's living presence at work in Christ and in the power of the Spirit will enable us rightly to participate in political life—with confidence yet humility, with a commitment to justice yet a suspicion of all political programs that promise to resolve every problem, and with gratitude for good government yet an awareness that the work of the church is never limited to politics but rather is concerned first of all with displaying God's reconciling and renewing power in its own life and in its ministries to the world.

FOR DISCUSSION

Concerns Raised in the Opening Dialogue

Should the church protest unjust government actions?
If the church takes a political stance, the church will just anger some of its members.
Shouldn't the church focus on spiritual, not worldly, things?
The gospel commands Christians to reach out to the weak and oppressed.

Questions

1. What are some of the views in your church about Christian involvement in politics?

2. How do the confessions challenge your personal views about the church and politics?
3. What fears do you have about talking about politics at church? How could a congregation or a session or a board of deacons raise these matters while respecting people's different points of view?
4. According to the confessions, what can we expect of government? What responsibilities does the church have for society, regardless of what the state does?

CONCLUSION

THE CHURCH LEADER
AS SPIRITUAL AND
THEOLOGICAL LEADER

Opening Prayer: *God of Grace and God of Glory, your Son taught us that others would know us by our fruits. May we receive the truth of the gospel not as a mere idea in our heads but rather as a way of life that brings forth deeper faithfulness to you and to others in the daily decisions that we make. We thank you for the example of our mothers and fathers in the faith. In Jesus' name, Amen.*[1]

Martha: I am glad we have been studying the confessions in order to prepare for our ordination as elders and deacons, but I still don't feel competent to teach others about them. Isn't that the pastor's job?

Jerry: Besides, we have a lot of practical decisions to make in the days ahead. I can see how the *Book of Order* and Robert's Rules of Order will guide us, but I'm not yet clear how we will use the *Book of Confessions*.

---

1. Based on chapter 1 of the Form of Government, "Preliminary Principles," G-1.0304.

Lisa: Still, I hope that we keep studying the Bible and the confessions at our meetings. That way if a member of the congregation asks me, "What do Presbyterians believe about baptism or the Lord's Supper?" or some other question, I know where to begin.

Max: The confessions remind me that a great cloud of witnesses from different times and places surrounds us. They inspire me to be more faithful to the work that God has given us to do.

This book has offered an overview of the most important teachings that run through the *Book of Confessions* as a whole. I have argued that despite their different historical contexts, audiences, and forms of expression, the confessions are remarkably consistent in their theological content. They establish reliable trajectories of belief along which we can continue to think the faith today. As we seek to communicate the gospel, we will not always use the confessions' language, but we cannot do without the confessions' wisdom. The church's confessions are more than curious museum pieces from the Reformed past; rather, they call us into deeper discipleship. They invite us to become better students of Scripture and more faithful witnesses to Christ, and they challenge us to confess the faith for ourselves and to others.

At the outset of the book, I noted that those called to office in the church—ministers, elders, and deacons alike—take vows to be instructed and led by the confessions and to accept their essential tenets. Knowledge of the confessions helps ministers, elders, and deacons serve more faithfully as the spiritual, theological leaders of the congregation. To be sure, normally only ministers receive formal seminary education. The church asks them to know the Scriptures and the church's theological traditions as well as possible, so that they may fulfill their special responsibilities for preaching, teaching, and leading worship. But we must not forget that elders and deacons are also called to think the faith as they lead a congregation and make practical decisions about its life and service. No less than ministers, elders and deacons are responsible to relate what we believe as Christians to what we do.

The essential connection between knowing and acting, thinking and doing, has been a key mark of our Reformed tradition. When Presbyterians first organized synods and a General Assembly in the newly independent United States, they included the following "historic principle of church order," which continues to appear as one of the preliminary principles of the church's Form of Government (G-1.0304):

> That truth is in order to goodness; and the great touchstone of truth, its tendency to promote holiness, according to our Savior's rule, "By their fruits ye shall know them." And that no opinion can be either more pernicious or more absurd than that which brings truth and falsehood upon a level, and represents it as of no consequence what a man's opinions are. On the contrary, we are persuaded that there is an inseparable connection between faith and practice, truth and duty. Otherwise, it would be of no consequence either to discover truth or to embrace it.

In an era sometimes called postmodern, truth seems elusive. We are aware of the many different points of view that shape our society and our churches. Different people seem to live by different truths and easily to move from one truth to another. Managing debate and difference in the church and in society can seem more important than resolving who is right or wrong or where the truth really lies. It is not surprising that church leaders are not always sure of their role on a session or a board of deacons.

The prominence of business models of leadership in contemporary America further complicates our understanding of church office. We are tempted to think of the pastor as an administrator or manager, with elders and deacons as their advisers and implementers. But then we begin to regard the church primarily as a social or business organization rather than as a body of believers who are called to discern what God is asking us to know and do.

A church that rediscovers its foundations in the confessions will think differently about church office. To be sure, the members of a session or a board of deacons will not always agree about the practical decisions that they make, and many of their decisions will seem no different from those of other organizations, such as how to maintain buildings, hire staff, and raise and spend money. These matters are not unimportant, and they often require managerial experience and business acumen. But attention to the confessions will remind church leaders that their first responsibilities are spiritual and theological.

Ministers are called to the service of the Word and the sacraments. What is the word of hope that a congregation or person needs at a particular moment? What will we preach as God's Word and not just our own? How can the sacraments invite us into a new way of life oriented by Christ's relationship to his Father?

Ruling elders are called to apply their "spiritual rulers" (measuring sticks) to the members of the congregation. Where are the people making progress in faith, and where are they falling short? What can assist them better to know and trust the God who has revealed himself in Jesus Christ?

Deacons are called to ministries of service and compassion. Who in the congregation or beyond is suffering, whether physically or spiritually? Who needs to hear that the God who rules all of history is also guiding their own life? Who needs a gesture of assistance that represents God's goodness to them personally?

The confessions will not give us direct answers for many of the decisions that a session or board of deacons face. But as the accumulated wisdom of the church, the confessions do remind us to seek God's will in whatever we do. They call us to remain rooted in what is most important of all: God's saving and transforming work in Jesus Christ for all humanity. When we have different perspectives on truth, we will turn to the confessions to see how they can help us read the Scriptures together, so that together we may better know Jesus as our living Lord and Savior.

Sessions and boards of deacons therefore have the special responsibility to make study of Scripture and the church's theological traditions as represented by the *Book of Confessions* an integral part of their work. Reflection on Scripture and important confessional teachings could constitute the first and major part of a "business" meeting; church leaders might take turns presenting their insights into a particular passage of the Bible and/or a confession and leading a discussion of what that passage means for a congregation's life.

Understanding the exercise of church office as a calling to spiritual, theological leadership can also help church nominating committees as they seek to identify candidates for a pastoral position, a session, or a board of deacons. Which candidates can help the congregation as a whole grow spiritually and theologically? Do these candidates already have a vital life of prayer? Do they practice disciplines of reading and reflecting on Scripture and the church's historic teachings? Are they prepared to grow in their capacity to listen to Scripture by learning from the church's confessions?

Spiritual, theological leadership places high demands on ministers, elders, and deacons, but no one exercises it alone. The Reformed tradition has affirmed that spiritual, theological leadership is shared among these offices. Ministers, elders, and deacons do not represent three ranks of power or prestige, but rather one body of church leadership with different functions. Church leaders take the same vows about trusting in Jesus Christ, accepting the Scriptures as the unique witness to him, and allowing the church's confessions to instruct, lead, and guide them as they lead the people of God. With the help of the confessions, church leaders and a congregation as a whole can enter more deeply into God's mission to the world.

"There is an inseparable connection between faith and practice, truth and duty." May the church's confessions be a precious resource for ministers, elders, deacons, and other church leaders as they call the people of God into witness, ministry, and service.

FOR DISCUSSION

Concerns Raised in the Opening Dialogue

Will elders and deacons ever feel confident enough to refer to the *Book of Confessions*?

The *Book of Order* seems more practical than the *Book of Confessions*.

How can the *Book of Confessions* help us know what we believe
   as Presbyterians?
Can the confessions inspire us to greater faithfulness?

Questions

1. What can you do as a church leader to be a spiritual and theological leader?
2. What are some ways in which your session or board of deacons might engage in ongoing study of the Bible and the confessions?
3. Why, for Christians, does truth matter?
4. What difference could the confessions make for the way in which a session or a board of deacons conducts its business?

APPENDIX

THE ORDINATION VOWS OF THE PRESBYTERIAN CHURCH (U.S.A.)

a. Do you trust in Jesus Christ your Savior, acknowledge him Lord of all and Head of the Church, and through him believe in one God, Father, Son, and Holy Spirit?

b. Do you accept the Scriptures of the Old and New Testaments to be, by the Holy Spirit, the unique and authoritative witness to Jesus Christ in the Church universal, and God's Word to you?

c. Do you sincerely receive and adopt the essential tenets of the Reformed faith as expressed in the confessions of our church as authentic and reliable expositions of what Scripture leads us to believe and do, and will you be instructed and led by those confessions as you lead the people of God?

d. Will you fulfill your office in obedience to Jesus Christ, under the authority of Scripture, and be continually guided by our confessions?

e. Will you be governed by our church's polity, and will you abide by its discipline? Will you be a friend among your colleagues in ministry, working with them, subject to the ordering of God's Word and Spirit?

f. Will you in your own life seek to follow the Lord Jesus Christ, love your neighbors, and work for the reconciliation of the world?

g. Do you promise to further the peace, unity, and purity of the church?

h. Will you seek to serve the people with energy, intelligence, imagination, and love?

i. (1) (For ruling elder) Will you be a faithful ruling elder, watching over the people, providing for their worship, nurture, and service? Will you share in government and discipline, serving in governing bodies of the church, and in your ministry will you try to show the love and justice of Jesus Christ?

(2) (For deacon) Will you be a faithful deacon, teaching charity, urging concern, and directing the people's help to the friendless and those in need? In your ministry will you try to show the love and justice of Jesus Christ?

(3) (For minister of the Word and Sacrament) Will you be a faithful minster of the Word and sacrament, proclaiming the good news in Word and Sacrament, teaching faith and caring for people? Will you be active in government and discipline, serving in governing bodies of the church, and in your ministry will you try to show the love and justice of Jesus Christ?

(4) (For commissioned pastor [also known as commissioned ruling elder]) Will you be a faithful ruling elder in this commission, serving the people by proclaiming the good news, teaching faith and caring for the people, and in your ministry will you try to show the love and justice of Jesus Christ?

(5) (For certified Christian educator) Will you be a faithful certified Christian educator, teaching faith and caring for people, and will you in your ministry try to show the love and justice of Jesus Christ?[1]

1. W-4.0404 (2017–19).

CPSIA information can be obtained
at www.ICGtesting.com
Printed in the USA
FSOW01n1026230118
43666FS